Everything Beautiful in Its Time

Jenna Bush Hager

Everything Beautiful in Its Time

Seasons of Love and Loss

WILLIAM MORROW
An Imprint of HarperCollins*Publishers*

Photograph on page 233 provided courtesy of the author.

Insert photographs provided courtesy of the author with the exception of the following: insert pages 2 and 3 courtesy of George H. W. Bush Library and Museum; insert pages 4, 8, 9, and 12 (top) by Paul Morse; insert pages 5, 13 (top), and 16 by Nathan Congleton; insert page 7 by Allison V. Smith; insert page 15 by Marlo Collins.

This is a work of nonfiction. The events and experiences detailed herein are all true and have been faithfully rendered as remembered by the author, to the best of her abilities. Some names have been changed to protect the privacy of the individuals involved.

HarperCollins books may be purchased for educational, business, or sales promotional use. For information please email the Special Markets Department at SPsales@harpercollins.com.

FIRST EDITION

Designed by Bonni Leon-Berman

Library of Congress Cataloging-in-Publication Data has been applied for.

ISBN 978-0-06-296062-7

20 21 22 23 24 LSC 10 9 8 7 6 5 4 3 2 1

TO HENRY,

my rock during the hard times

and the beautiful ones

Contents

My Four Grandparents

At my paternal grandparents' house in Maine, on the back of every door my grandmother posted a typed page of house rules. With seventeen grandchildren and eight great-grandchildren running around, my Ganny, First Lady Barbara Bush, wanted to make clear what she expected of us. These rules were simple, practical guidelines for keeping the house running smoothly, but they also taught us respect.

> Don't track in sand.
> Hang up your towel.
> Tell us if you'll be eating dinner out.
> Make your bed.

My grandfather, President George H. W. Bush, whom I called Gampy, had a list of guidelines for us, too. They were words of advice for living a life of passion and meaning, their humility and kindness as familiar as the loop in the cursive of his handwriting.

Don't get down when your life takes a bad turn.
Don't blame others for your setbacks.
When things go well, always give credit to others.
Don't talk all the time. Listen to your friends and
    mentors and learn from them.
Don't brag about yourself. Let others point out your
    virtues, your strong points.
Give someone a hand. When a friend is hurting,
    show that friend you care.
Nobody likes an overbearing big shot.
As you succeed, be kind to people. Thank those who
    help you along the way.
Don't be afraid to shed a tear when your heart is
    broken or because a friend is hurting.

My maternal grandparents don't have airports or
schools named after them. Jenna and Harold Welch,
whom I called Grammee and Pa, worked as a housewife
and a home builder. They never posted rules on doors.
And yet I watched them live by their own codes, and I
learned from them.

Don't be intimidated by people who have a better
    education or more money. Kindness is more
    valuable than any fortune.
Smile at every baby you see.
Regardless of what you do, be proud of working hard
    to take care of your family.
Read widely.

If anyone spills something, yell "Happy days!" It
   reminds everyone not to sweat the small stuff.
Get out of bed to go look at the stars—and always,
   always wish upon the first star you see.

My Pa left us in 1995 after a struggle with Alzheimer's, but all three of my other grandparents have died
in the past thirteen months—my Ganny on April 17,
2018; Gampy on November 30, 2018; my Grammee on
May 10, 2019.

I know how fortunate I was to have them for so long.
And yet the knowledge that they had long, happy lives
did not make the goodbyes any less sad. This year has
been one of the most profound of my life, full of both
glorious love and terrible loss.

Consolation has come from sharing their words and
stories with family, friends, and anyone else who will listen. I've learned so much from the examples set by all
four of my grandparents, and I'm lucky that they were all
prolific letter writers. I find solace in rereading the letters
they sent me over the years; I share my favorites in this
book.

In the midst of grief, life has continued. My husband,
Henry Hager, and I have two little daughters, Poppy and
Mila, now four and six. They are our greatest joy, but also
our greatest challenge. The same week I got a promotion at work, I found out I was pregnant with our third
child, Hal. He was born in August, bringing more happiness and more chaos to a household already bursting

with both. I only wish his great-grandparents had lived to meet him.

As long as I'm alive, my grandparents will not be forgotten. I'll tell their stories to my children so that their spirits live on in our family. And they will be by my side as I walk through life. I hear their voices in the letters they sent me and in my memories. They offer comfort, support, and guidance, and I will listen to them always.

Hiding from My Favorite People on Earth

Dearest Mila and Poppy,

This is a letter about motherhood, a word you don't yet truly understand. Sure, you say the word *Mama* countless times a day—a word I will never tire of hearing. But motherhood—and the unconditional love and longing (and anxiety and guilt) that come along with it—is something you won't know about for many years.

My mama, your Grammee, is one of the all-time greats. She always put us first; she was calm and patient even when we tested her. I watched her "mother" for many years, but it wasn't until you were born that I understood what motherhood means. And it wasn't until I held you—with Grammee by my hospital bed—that I really understood my mom.

You come from a long line of women who desperately wanted to be mothers. The West Texas women on your grandma's side were strong, but all the way back to my great-grandmother, the thing they wanted the most was the most difficult. Both your grandma and my grandma Jenna (for whom I'm named) are only children—and not by choice. My great-grandmother, a woman who could make her own mortar and lay her own brick, buried at least two babies in the deserts of El Paso, both born too soon. And my grandma Jenna laid three babies to rest in Midland, Texas.

Your grandparents, my parents, wanted a full household and tried to have children for many years before putting in an application to adopt. The day they found out they had been accepted by the adoption agency was the day they found out they were pregnant with your aunt Barbara and me. Later, when I was a teenager, your Grammee gave me their picture from the adoption form, framed. "Doesn't this look like two people who wanted to be parents?" she said. I've kept that picture by my bed, a reminder of their love.

It is a reminder I have never needed; life with our mom was filled with love. After baths every night, hair wet, pajama-clad, we danced around the house to the Pointer Sisters' "Fire." A conga line of Bush women: the two of us following in our mama's footsteps. We always followed her lead. Your Grammee took us on trips, just the three of us, to see Frida Kahlo and other art exhibits across Texas (long before your grandpa was into art!). She wanted us to see the beauty in the world.

Now people will say, "You remind me so much of your mom!" and I thank them. It is the best compliment. In many ways, I am like her: our voices ring with the same Texas twang; we have similar cheekbones; we were both teachers and love to read. But in many ways, I am just trying to keep up with her.

It is my mama who taught me how to be a mom, but it is you, my darlings, who are teaching me what it means to be a mom. When I hold you at night, singing the same songs your Grammee sang to me, I am filled with unconditional love. It is a new feeling, but one I know my parents always felt for Barbara and me. When I am traveling for work, I scroll through pictures of you on my phone, longing to be back home.

Your Grammee prepared me for the anxiety and guilt that come with motherhood. She said recently, "All we know we have is now, so worry less and enjoy life with those babies."

So I do that now. And I think about my strong mama and my grandmas—the women who came before—and I'm so grateful you are mine.

Just like those moments dancing years ago, feet
in rhythm to my mama's step, I am following her
lead again. And I am dancing with the two of you as
often as I can.
Love,
Mama

I wrote this letter to my girls when they were babies,
and I also ended the last book I wrote, *Sisters First*, by
saying I would never tire of hearing the word *Mama*.
At the time, I believed that with all that I am. Whenever
Mila, then four years old, held my hand and gazed up at
me, uttering, "Mama," I felt a surge of pure love. Every
time my puppy-eyed baby Poppy said the word—after, of
course, the easier-to-say "Dada"—my heart soared.

And yet, after the haze and euphoria of holding my
beautiful babies in my arms faded, I wasn't entirely prepared for the mundane moments of parenthood: the
maddening tasks, the arguing, the negotiating over food
and frocks. Now, two years later, I can name the exact
moment when the word *Mama* lost its luster.

It had been a long day. I was finally in the bathtub at
home, decompressing.

"Mama!" I heard Mila yell from the living room. "Can
you bring us water? We're thirsty!"

"Ask Daddy!" I called back. Henry was sitting on the
couch next to them, willing and able to serve.

"Water!" she repeated. "Mama!"

That was it. That was the moment when the word lost a little of its sheen.

WHEN MILA WAS three and a half, my mom was in town visiting. The three of us went out shopping. The first part of the day was lovely. We strolled. We snacked. We people-watched. We talked to Mila about the pigeons and the squirrels.

And then in an instant our idyllic outing took a turn. Mila went limp and boneless. Somehow, in spite of her floppiness, she was able to ferociously kick the pavement with her tiny sneakered feet and to chop the air with her little hands. The trigger for all this rage? Her grandmother and mother wouldn't buy her a pink pig watch at a store. My mom and I are both of the school that you don't give in to tantrums, so we moved away from that store and tried to get back to my apartment. We used every toddler parenting trick, including redirection: *Look, another squirrel!*

"Mama, Mama, Mama!" Mila screamed over and over, like a human robocall.

I cringed. My mom cringed. The black-suited Secret Service agents following my mom cringed. Their job is to keep my mom inconspicuous. Mila was not helping. At all.

People looked up from their phones and stared at the adorable little girl who seemed to be in serious distress.

Then they looked at the little girl's elegant grandmother, the former First Lady, in her neat sweater set.

They also saw the frazzled mother, an overwhelmed thirtysomething woman whose hair was a mess and who was clearly in the wrong. If I had been one of these strangers, I might have judged me, too.

On that city sidewalk, there was no place to hide. But other times, there *are* hiding spots, and I take advantage of them. Once when the children's witching hour, that dinner-to-sleep window, was coming to a close, I put the girls in bed. We'd read books, brushed teeth, gotten water, read more books, said prayers. I stood in the kitchen, utterly exhausted, eating the girls' string cheese for dinner.

I heard Poppy call out, "Mama, Mama, Mama!" as she escaped from her bed for the hundredth time. I was briefly reminded of something my father used to say: "There's nothing you can do to make me stop loving you, so *stop trying so hard.*"

I should have run to Poppy immediately, I know. Instead, I stepped into the pantry and pulled the door closed, so during those few seconds before she came running into the kitchen and found me, I could finish the last strand of my cheese stick in peace.

Sister Love
and Sister Strife

When we were seven, my sister and I began an annual tradition of traveling from Dallas to Midland, Texas (a one-hour flight), to visit our Pa and Grammee. We felt so sophisticated on that first trip when our mom kissed us goodbye and we walked onto the plane by ourselves under the watchful eye of the flight attendant.

On this first unchaperoned flight, my sister and I got into a terrible fight—one that I may or may not have instigated. Barbara, tears in her eyes, arms folded, made it clear that she never wanted to see or speak to me again. She could not wait to get off the plane so we could part ways forever.

At just that moment, a male passenger leaned over to Barbara and, gesturing at me, said, "Are you going to spank her or should I?"

Instantly Barbara transferred her rage from me to this stranger who had just threatened her beloved sister. We had a new common enemy, and our fight was forgotten. By the time we walked off the plane in Midland toward our waiting grandparents, we were holding hands.

Since the publication of *Sisters First*, which Barbara and I wrote about the joys of sisterhood, people often ask us, "Didn't you *ever* fight?" At one tour stop, a woman said, "Am I doing something wrong? My twins are always fighting!" At another, a woman said, "I fight with my sister constantly. I love her, but we are always arguing. How can we be more like you two?"

To set the record straight, we are not magically peaceful siblings; as children we fought often. Once when we were thirteen, changing clothes in a baseball stadium bathroom for an opening-day game, I threw a Steve Madden chunky-heeled mule—this was the 1990s; they were very in—at my sister. I watched as the shoe flew through the air as if in slow motion and made contact with her head. I panicked when she started *bleeding* from her scalp.

"I'm so sorry!" I said. *Had I permanently damaged my sister? Would she need stitches? Would she have a scar?* Embarrassingly, more important to me in that moment: *When it was discovered, would my parents ground me?*

Once it was clear that the wound was superficial and the patient would live, I segued into damage control: "If you tell Mom and Dad, I'm going to tell them about what you did last week . . ."

The truth was, we both had indiscretions to hide. I may have had the advantage of size and strength, but Barbara was scrappy. I might punch, but she had strong nails and wasn't afraid to use them.

I remember many physical and verbal fights, but I don't remember what a single one was about. They were about everything and nothing, probably. I do know they were never about boys. We favor very different romantic types. Growing up, Barbara always liked a guy with a tattoo and a little edge. I dated the class president. I think more than anything else our fights were the result of a clash of temperaments, of the way we move differently through the world.

I see this difference in one way or another nearly every time we are together. For example, during our book tour, we had just boarded a plane and put our bags away when Barbara spotted someone a few rows up and grabbed my arm. "Look!" she said. "It's Bryan Stevenson, founder of the Equal Justice Initiative!"

I had read about his work, but I wouldn't have been able to recognize him. Barbara, meanwhile, knew who it was from glimpsing his partial profile.

"He does such great work!" she said. She went on to give me his full résumé, down to naming wrongfully incriminated people he had freed. She finished by saying, "I have to go and thank him."

At this point, passengers were still boarding the plane. Anyone who has flown recently knows that going against the tide is a dangerous proposition. There was no room in the aisle, but she stood up, intent on making her way toward him.

"Are you really going to go now?" I asked her. "People are still boarding the plane. You'll get crushed. You can thank him after we take off. At least wait until everyone's on b—"

Before I had finished my plea, she was already halfway down the aisle, moving rapidly, like a salmon swimming upstream. I watched in horror as my thin twin sister was almost taken out five times by rolling bags being thrust into overhead bins. Then I heard her greet him and say, shaking his hand, "Thank you so much for your work. It inspires me in everything I do."

When she came back I said, "Barbara, I can't believe you just did that."

"I needed to thank him for what he does," she said, as if there were no choice but to have spoken to him that very minute. "It's not easy work, and I think it's always best to thank people right when you see them."

When people ask me, "What's your sister like?" I think about moments like that. She's all heart—and all action.

But Barbara's also a dreamer. On the phone recently, she was going on about plans for a trip we were about to take; I told her, not very sensitively, that I thought she was trying to do too much. She snapped at me and hung up.

At just that moment, a young woman stopped me on the sidewalk to say she loved *Sisters First*.

"I live in this building with my sister!" she said, pointing across the street. Then, sounding ashamed, she whispered, "We're in a fight."

"Hey, me too!" I said. "My sister and I are also in a fight!"

We both laughed, secure in the knowledge that fighting is part of sisterhood. Fortunately, so is making up, and so is being there when it counts most.

Not long after Poppy was born, Barbara and I took a quick trip to Oklahoma to promote our book. As I discovered to my dismay a few hours into the trip, I couldn't get my breast pump to work. Barbara is handy, a born architect, but even she couldn't fix the contraption. We had to drive to Babies "R" Us—me wailing about my giant, swollen boobs the whole way—to rent a pump. She was there for me on that uncomfortable day, and I've been there for her over the years, too.

I've watched as my sister's heart has been bruised by breakups and was broken when her teenage boyfriend died. When Barbara's heart hurts, mine does, too. That is a bond that no fight can breach—nails or no nails.

This has proved true even though we've taken different paths. In the past decade, I've gotten married and had children as she stayed single.

Our differences showed themselves early. As a little girl, I was fascinated with Barbies. I woke up early to play with my Barbies before I left for school. I even—to save time—played with them while on the toilet, the fourth grader's version of reading the newspaper. My dad bought me a hot-pink DO NOT DISTURB sign with Barbie on it that he put on my bathroom door. I played for hours, creating typically romantic scenarios. My favorites were the torrid love triangles in which Barbie eventually ended up with Ken. Every morning, as the sun rose over suburban Dallas, I managed to cram an entire season's worth of soap opera drama into that bathroom.

I also loved bridal magazines. I studied the dresses, flower arrangements, and cakes as if I were preparing for a standardized test. The fact that I didn't marry the first boy I met after I turned eighteen is a miracle—though at twenty-six I *was* pretty close!

My sister played with the same Barbies and flipped through the same magazines, though in both cases with less enthusiasm than I did. Did she dream of marriage as a little girl? Probably. But as we got older, her ideas about love changed. Her huge heart had room for more than just a man.

In our mid-thirties, I faced constant questions about my sister's love life—namely, her lack of a spouse. On our book tour, I was struck by how often she was asked when she was getting married and how often I was asked to account for why she wasn't married yet. She was accomplished in countless ways, and yet no one ever seemed to ask about her life-changing work in Africa.

At one tour stop, in Palo Alto, California, Condoleezza Rice moderated a conversation between Barbara and me. She asked what questions we heard most often.

"I get asked, 'When is your sister getting married?'" I said. "It's 2018! Isn't it time we asked women different questions?"

Condi paused and then said, "I still get asked why I didn't get married."

I was appalled. She was the former secretary of state! Shouldn't we ask her about Russia? Putin? She has been a professor, an author, and a concert pianist. She is a good golfer and loves football. How is it possible that strong, accomplished women are mainly being asked about their love lives?

I believe that love comes when it is supposed to; I saw it happen for my beloved sister when we were on our book tour.

When we arrived in Atlanta, my sister began texting with someone named Craig Coyne. Friends had long been trying to set them up, but every time they got close to an actual encounter, something had kept them from meeting. This day they were supposed to have coffee, but Barbara and I, exhausted from touring, had discovered the hotel's "welcome bag," overflowing with Doritos and Pringles. Before we knew it, we'd crawled into the giant bed we were sharing and begun watching a movie—then another movie.

Having eaten nothing but orange-colored food all day, Barbara was in a hotel-room slough of despondency and not eager for the pressure of a first date. Right as she was about to cancel, I told her that she should invite Craig for a casual group drink at the hotel bar that night. A college friend and I were meeting that evening and they could join us. She resisted, but as she was weakened by her Doritos coma, I wore her down.

At the bar downstairs, Barbara went up to three different men asking if they were Craig, only to be told no. The fourth candidate—and to her delight by far the most handsome of all the potential Craigs—was the right one. He sat at our table, and right away it was clear to everyone there that he and Barbara had chemistry.

Earlier that day, Barbara had made me swear that I wouldn't invite him to our book event, no matter how well the drinks were going. I am usually true to my word. But this was a moment when I took it upon myself to break my promise.

When I asked Craig if he would like to come to our talk that evening, Barbara dealt me a sharp elbow to the ribs. Craig, ignoring my yelp of pain, said he would love to. After we finished our drinks, we headed to the Marcus Jewish Community Center of Atlanta.

The MJCCA venue seated hundreds of people and it was oversold. Our moderator was Emily Giffin, the Atlanta author of, yes, romantic comedies. No one loves a marriage plot and romance more than Emily Giffin, and she was very happy to learn that Barbara and Craig were on their first date.

While we were onstage talking, Emily told the crowd that Craig was on a blind date with Barbara. Barbara groaned. Craig blushed. Emily doubled down and asked for the spotlight to shine on him sitting in the audience. Fortunately, the tech crew did not know what Craig looked like and put the wrong man in the spotlight's glare. After the talk, Emily insisted we all take a photo together.

"This way when you two get married, you can look at this picture and remember the night you first met!"

Craig and Barbara laughed.

Then, just six months later, they did just that.

They would have waited longer to wed, but my grandmother had just died and they wanted my grandfather to be at the wedding. We held the ceremony that October in Maine, under the changing maple and beech trees. I was thrilled to watch Barbara marry her true love, especially because watching proudly, a blanket over his lap, was our ninety-four-year-old Gampy.

The wedding was intimate, just twenty family members. It took place where Barbara and I played as little girls, pretending the rocks along the coast were pirate ships. My grandfather spent every summer at this place, except when he was fighting in World War II. It was on these same rocks that he had proposed to our Ganny.

The day of the wedding was cold and overcast but beautiful. Mila was the flower girl; Poppy, the ring bearer. Poppy had been given an empty box to prevent her losing the actual rings, and during her entire trip down the aisle she repeatedly gestured toward the box, informing the guests, "It's a fake! It's a fake!"

As I walked down the aisle, smiling at Gampy, I was reminded of how eleven years earlier he'd walked down the aisle at my wedding. He'd just begun to show symptoms of Parkinson's and had grown unsteady on his feet. As he walked toward the altar on our family ranch, wearing a beautiful seersucker suit, he slipped on the wet grass and stumbled. Catching himself, he gestured toward his blue-and-white suit and said, "Seersucker is back!"

At our ceremony, he read the passage "When I was a child, I spoke as a child." At age eighty-four, he looked at once powerful and frail.

On Barbara's wedding day, our aunt Dorothy Bush Koch—Aunt Doro to Barbara and me—who embodies the same quiet decency as her father, presided. As soon as the brief, lovely ceremony concluded, it started raining. I joked that it was a sign Ganny was upset that we moved the furniture around so we could have a cocktail hour inside.

We ate a big dinner at the same table where we'd had countless meals in the years before. Gampy sat in between Barbara and me. The last words he ever spoke to her were "You have never been more beautiful."

At that dinner, I stood up to toast her. As I did, I looked in her eyes and realized that my earliest, greatest love—the person who taught me the most about being in a partnership—had been just down the hall of our three-bedroom ranch house growing up: my sister, with her narrow shoulders, tortoiseshell glasses, and thick-as-rope auburn hair.

I want to toast my beautiful, closest Barbara on the night of her wedding. Tonight, guided by the ocean, the soundtrack of our childhood, you married sweet Craig. In this place that has been an anchor for us—where we crabbed as toddlers with Dad in the "Booney wild pool," played Sardines with our cousins, read nightly in our Ganny's lap, and recently read to Gampy—you started your own family.

Barbara, I have loved you every moment of our lives. Having you as my life partner has been one of the greatest gifts of my life.

It isn't surprising that I've loved you—Craig knows, we all do. Barbara is easy to love. I was slightly harder, but, Barbara, you have loved me with patience and grace every day.

People ask a lot: Have you always been so close? And the answer: an easy yes. I have proof. Here is a picture of us as toddlers where I am loving Barbara so ferociously there is a red mark on her neck. My love was not always as gentle as hers.

Craig, having Barbara by your side will make you braver than you ever thought possible. Right here as toddlers we wanted to play by the sea at night, so we escaped our cribs. We were apprehended on the ten-foot seawall and escorted by the Secret Service to our parents, who were eating at this very table. This was the first time we were in trouble with the law. Not the last.

Barbara's name means "beautiful stranger." We learned this at an airport, from a key chain, and we loved it. It seemed so grown-up. And appropriate in some ways: her beauty is obvious, and she's elusive.

But the description isn't exactly correct. Barbara has never met a stranger she didn't embrace. Just ask

Tequila, from our first grade class, or Josephine, her Swedish best friend she met in Italy. Or ask the little girl in Rwanda in a lavender dress living with HIV, who would change Barbara's life. Or Heather, Katie, Mama B, Ruth, or James—any number of the thousands of people in Rwanda, Uganda, Newark. This is one reason I'm so proud you're my sister. And everyone at this table is proud to know you, B.

There is one person we are missing—whose seat is impossible to fill—who would be beaming with pride, and that is our Ganny. She would be thrilled by this wedding. She adored her namesake. And Junior, as Gampy calls her, is more like her namesake than you may guess. Barbara Junior lives with the same strength and compassion that our Ganny lived with.

And the strength part—well, Craig, that's where you come in. You may need some, entering into this family. Just ask Henry—or Hank, as my Gampy and now the whole family calls him. But, Craigie Baby, as Poppy calls you—it is your kindness and empathy that make you a perfect life partner for my life partner. Henry has been the ham in this family sandwich for fifteen years, and he is more than thrilled that he now has you to be . . . the mayo? Swiss cheese? Choose your filling.

And so, to toast the two of you, I wanted to find words from a great romantic on love, devotion, and commitment. Shakespeare and Neruda weren't doing the trick. Turns out the perfect words were written by the great romantic Gampy, to our Ganny.

January 6, 1994
For: Barbara Pierce
From: GHWB

Will you marry me? Oops, I forgot, you did that 49 years ago today! I was very happy on that day in 1945, but I am even happier today. You have given me joy that few men know. You have made our boys into men by bawling them out and then, right away, by loving them. You have helped Doro be the sweetest, greatest daughter in the whole wide world. I have climbed perhaps the highest mountain in the world, but even that cannot hold a candle to being Barbara's husband. Mum used to tell me: "Now, George, don't walk ahead." Little did she know I was only trying to keep up—keep up with Barbara Pierce from Onondaga Street in Rye, New York. I love you!

This is what I wish for you: the laughter, devotion, and adoration they felt for each other. The respect and, most of all, the compassion. Craig, I hope in fifty years you're writing a love letter like this to Barbara. Oh, and, Craig—good luck keeping up with Barbara Pierce Bush from Texas.

A Letter from Ganny on Barbara's and My Birthday

November 30, 2011

Dearest Jenna and Barbara,

After I heard that Henry (a thoughtful great loving man) gave Gampy's letter to you early, I felt I could relax and get my letter to you nearer to the actual birthday. So many things to debate. Do I write separate letters? Or do I write one letter to you both? You certainly are two distinctive wonderful people and yet you are closer than any two people I know. So one letter. Maybe this is lazy. It is lazy.

Random thoughts:

God was good to you in that you are so different in physical appearance (both lovely looking), you are both smart and bright, your interests are different and your friends are the same and different, also. And friends . . . you girls have more fabulous friends and you have shared some of them with us. Thank you for that. "Friends are friends forever," as Michael W. Smith's song says. How true.

I don't know if I was supposed to write about your growing pains as normal young people growing up in an abnormal political world. You had them. So what!

Among other things thanks to an amazing mother and father with the patience of saints who set a good example, and especially your own discipline, you have grown into absolutely wonderful caring, giving, loving people. Gampy and I are so proud of you and love you more than you will ever know.
Love and more love,
Ganny

Do Not Speak
to Me of "Balance"

My parents showed us unconditional love, and they spent a lot of time with us. My mom drove car pool in our baby-blue minivan with wood paneling. When we were in elementary school, our dad left work daily in time to get home for a run while I rode my bike next to him. We had family game nights to play our favorite, Sorry!, and went to more baseball games than we could count. Sure, there was discipline, but my parents were more likely to find our irreverence amusing than to punish us for it.

When I was three and we were selling our Midland, Texas, home, the only house I'd ever known, I rode my tricycle in tight, menacing circles around the prospective buyers. It was not polite behavior, and yet my mother thought it was charming that I was a toddler homebody who did not approve of strangers invading our house.

In my parents' home, when we made mistakes as little

people, then later as big people, we experienced their infinite mercy and forgiveness. They never expected perfection. Once we were in the White House, our parents continued to forgive some missteps. There is no guide for being a First Daughter.

I would find it hard to be a parent if I held myself to an impossible standard of perfection. When people ask me how I balance work and small children, I say, "It's simple. I don't." I've been blessed with a lot of wonderful things at once. I don't want to give anything up, so I keep everything going the best I can.

Am I balanced? Of course not. As I write this, I'm at my desk at work surrounded by coffee cups. By my side is a purse that contains Chuck E. Cheese tokens and . . . an old lollipop that Poppy wanted to save for later, now stuck to an important work document.

People never ask men how they manage to balance work and family. It's woman-focused terminology, designed to make us feel bad about ourselves. What's more, I find the question of balance to be a signifier of privilege. Such questions are inherently elitist. The moms of the kids I taught in D.C. and Baltimore never indulged in such questions. They were worried about bills and their paychecks and their children's well-being. With their free time after work, they focused on applying to programs so their kids had chances they didn't.

When Amy Schumer did a stand-up set just a couple of weeks after giving birth, some moms shamed her for it. She posted a photo of herself with her breast pump, looking utterly exhausted and vulnerable, and sent it out to all the moms trying to make her feel bad. That morning on *Today*, Savannah Guthrie and I praised Schumer for defending herself. We agreed that if a mom takes a couple of hours out of the house in those first weeks, it can help keep her sane.

I surround myself with women who are flawed and hilarious and don't take themselves too seriously. On a recent vacation with Savannah and her family, I got a lesson in parenting humility. It began idyllically. Everything you hear about the closeness of the *Today* show family is real. Every year, Savannah and I take the kids up to her place in the country. It's on these trips that I understand the value of a village raising a child. You can go for a walk alone while another mom watches your children; then you can watch them all while she goes to the store.

On this trip, in the dead of winter, a thick layer of snow covered the ground. One afternoon I was upstairs taking a nap while Poppy and Mila were hanging out with Savannah's two children and some other kids. Suddenly, the whole gang burst into my room, all yelling at once, in hysterics: "Poppy has eaten an adult pill!"

This is not my favorite way to wake up from a nap. I immediately went into reporter mode. Quickly I learned that Poppy was not about to start hallucinating. She had just eaten one of the other kids' chocolate-flavored laxatives. Unlike that child, Poppy is regular and does not need a laxative. As that weekend progressed, she must have asked every person at the house to wipe her.

My first day back from winter vacation, I felt I had achieved my perfect ideal of the balanced life. It was the first Monday of the new year. My productivity was at its peak, my diet still intact. I began my day with a green juice. I had a thousand meetings set up. I was wearing high-heeled boots instead of flats. New year, new you!

At my fifth meeting of the day, I was on a high of checking things off my to-do list. My goals were growing loftier by the minute. To my meeting companions, I was listing all the things I would do. Frankly, I was an inspiration even to myself.

As I made a sweeping gesture with my arm, I caught a glimpse of my watch. It was 3:40.

Mila gets off the bus at 3:45.

I stood up and told the people I was meeting with why I'd just gone pale, then shrieked, "What do I do? My daughter gets off the school bus in five minutes and I'm picking her up!"

Then I looked at Google Maps and saw that I was 0.9 miles away from the pickup spot. Traffic was terrible, so a cab was out. My conclusion: "I have to run."

My colleagues wished me luck as I sprinted down the hall.

Out on the street, it was a freezing January afternoon, but I didn't feel the cold because I was running at top speed. I now regretted the high-heeled boots.

"You'll make it!" strangers called out as I ran in a panic. "Don't worry! You're okay!"

"No!" I called back. "I'm not okay! None of this is okay!"

I grew up in suburban Dallas. We carpooled or rode our bikes home from Preston Hollow Elementary. Now I was envisioning my five-year-old daughter, who just started her second semester of kindergarten, getting off the bus on a corner in lower Manhattan, standing there shivering like the Little Match Girl in front of Duane Reade.

Fortunately, I ran track in school. Unfortunately, I was a lousy runner. I often came in last and once faked a hamstring injury when I realized the race was lost (and not just by a little), because it was just too humiliating to lose every time without some extenuating circumstances.

Now, though, I was fast enough that I arrived at the bus stop, breathing very heavily, in almost no time at all—my feet aching, my mind racing, my shame spiraling!

My baby was not standing there on the corner whimpering. Had she already been kidnapped? As I contemplated dialing 911, the bus pulled up. It was blessedly late—due to the traffic caused, no doubt, by all those suddenly productive New Yorkers. It was late on the very day I needed it to be late, which is just the type of serendipitous thing that rarely happens.

That was the best wake-up call I could have gotten in the new year. In my zeal to check everything off my to-do list, I'd forgotten what was most important.

Another wake-up call came when Poppy asked me this question as I was putting her in her cotton pajamas: "Mommy, is there a babysitter, or are you going to be babysitting us tonight?"

"You know I don't babysit you," I said. "I'm your mom."

To which she responded, "Okay, Mom, are you *mothering* us tonight?"

Oh no. Was I going to be *mothering* them tonight?

In fact, I was supposed to go out. But what was I supposed to say to my baby: "No, no mothering for you"?

"Yes, I will be mothering you," I said, as I picked up the phone to cancel my plans.

The Wrong Movie

If you'd asked me twenty years ago if I would one day pursue a career in media, I would have said absolutely not. This was the industry that had plastered "freshman fifteen" photos of Barbara and me everywhere after we were caught drinking underage. And yet for a full year when I was in my mid-twenties, a producer at the *Today* show kept calling to ask if I would consider coming on as a correspondent.

For many months, the answer was a firm no. The press were not my friends. My students and fellow teachers were. I had just finished another year as an English teacher at a school in Baltimore. I had also written a couple of books: *Ana's Story*, about a teenage mother with AIDS whom I'd met working for UNICEF, and a children's book, cowritten with my mother, called *Read All About It!*

In the course of that year, however, I'd lost a bit of my resolve to continue teaching. I loved my classes, and yet teaching in inner-city Baltimore was difficult. We'd gone through several principals in one year. I worked fifteen-, sixteen-hour days. I wondered if I'd be able to do the job for decades without burning out.

That summer I was in Maine with my grandparents, on my own with them for the first time ever. We have a huge family of cousins, aunts, and uncles. For once, it was just them and me. How fortunate I felt to glow alone in their spotlight.

One night as we finished our dinner of swordfish and corn, I told them about the job offer from the *Today* show. I told them that I was conflicted about exploring the opportunity. In Baltimore, I was fulfilling my dream of making a difference as an educator. But maybe there was a way I could make a difference on TV? I asked what they thought.

"Why don't you at least take the interview?" Ganny said. "It is always a good idea to take the meeting."

It might surprise people to hear that, because my Ganny had a reputation for being a traditionalist. Henry and I were newlyweds. She never was shy about her en-thusiasm for more great-grandchildren.

The truth is, she was more progressive than people gave her credit for. On the one hand, she dropped out of Smith College to get married and had been known to en-courage women with small children to stay home (though she never put that pressure on me). On the other hand, she had accomplished a great deal on her own, particularly when it came to her work in literacy. She once ended a talk at a women's college with this: "And who knows? Somewhere out in this audience may even be someone who will one day follow in my footsteps, and preside over the White House as the president's spouse. I wish him well!"

As had happened with a lot of my Ganny's rules, I think over time her thoughts on women working had shifted. She never told me not to work and in fact sent me letters of encouragement while I was teaching. In one, she wrote, "Dear Jenna—*Among Schoolchildren* by Tracy Kidder [a book I had given her] reminds me so of you. . . . Do you have a Clarence or a Robert in your class? What a challenge for you! . . . We miss you and are so proud of you."

By the time we were eating our dessert of blueberry pie, I'd resolved to take my grandmother's advice. I would take the meeting.

THE NEXT DAY, as the early-morning Maine sun streamed through the windows, I sipped my coffee on the couch. My grandfather, sitting beside me, the morning papers in his lap, said, "Do you ever watch the *Today* show? Why don't we turn it on?"

That was my Gampy. He had a smart, practical, and obvious strategy for deciding on whether I wanted the job: learning more about what it would entail. That simple act hadn't even occurred to me (not that it was an option during the school year, because I was off to work before the show even began).

The three of us sat on their little blue sofa and turned on NBC. We watched and talked, drinking coffee. Then we saw Matt Lauer and Sacha Baron Cohen seated opposite each other on the morning-show set. Cohen was promoting *Brüno*, the movie in which he pretends to be "an international man of fashion."

While Cohen, in character as Brüno, perched dramatically on his chair in a silver jumpsuit and silly little hat, Lauer asked him whose idea it had been to wear a Velcro suit backstage at a fashion show. (A clip showed the slapstick chaos that followed, as a large black backdrop and an entire rack of clothes stuck to him.) His reply: "Why did *ich* do it? Why do artists do anything? Why did Louis Armstrong walk on ze moon? Why did Caesar build Rome in a day? Why did Leonardo DiCaprio paint the *Mona Lisa*? *Ich* don't know."

We heard the morning-show crew laughing in the background. In Maine, we guffawed.

The interview had us captivated. My grandparents and I hadn't heard much about the film, but the hilarity of the TV interview drew us to the theater. Gampy and I decided to see a screening that very afternoon.

It was a perfect day, not a cloud in the sky. We usually went to the movies only when the Maine sky turned dark gray and the wind whipped up, but on that glorious summer day we drove, accompanied as ever by Gampy's Secret Service, to the movie theater in Portland, Maine.

My grandpa was in his eighties. He believed in a high level of decorum. If you've seen the film, or even parts of it, you can imagine how awkward this experience was for the former leader of the free world. And now imagine that at your side is your twenty-six-year-old granddaughter, who had greatly encouraged this outing. I sunk down in my seat, laughing more at the absurdity of our predicament than at the movie.

On the screen, Brüno stripped to his underwear and made a pass at Congressman Ron Paul in a hotel room. He took a karate class to learn how to fend off an attack by sex toys. He adopted a baby, hoping to emulate Angelina Jolie, and picked it up from a box at baggage claim.

Within minutes, Gampy was visibly uncomfortable. Listening to risqué jokes while sitting next to my elderly grandfather—jokes that in another context I might have found funny—made me blush scarlet.

"What should we do?" my grandfather whispered to me. "Should we get up?"

"I don't know," I whispered back.

"How are we going to walk out of here without attracting attention?" he said.

We stayed through the whole thing and then sheepishly snuck out.

Of course, I did not hold our misbegotten trip to see *Brüno* against the *Today* show. Thanks to my grandparents' encouragement, I did take the meeting, and then I took the job. This year, I celebrated my ten-year anniversary at NBC. And every time I recommend a book or film on the air, I make sure to tell viewers whether it's something they should share with their children or their elders.

Out There
on the Water

When Barbara and I were little, our parents bought a small cabin on Rainbo Lake in East Texas. The area was known as a paradise for outdoor sportsmen. The lake was teeming with bass, and the piney woods were full of deer. Barbara and I were thrilled—at first. Then we learned that we were not allowed to swim in the lake because it was filled with giant alligators. At best, our parents let us jump in for a fast dip if the heat was particularly oppressive. Then we had to pop back out again before the alligators noticed their next meal.

The main activity at the lake was to fish from our fishing boat, which was big enough to accommodate several people. My father and my grandfather loved the sport of it. Both of them were gentlemen and gentle fishermen. They were always catch-and-release guys. The meticulous act of calmly disengaging the fish from the perilous hook seemed as important to them as the casting.

Fishing was never my sport. The pace was too slow. When I put my line in the water, I scared the fish away. Barbara and I were always looking for adventure, trying to make those fishing trips more than they were. We brought many distractions with us onto the boat to keep ourselves entertained: books, Barbies, board games. When I was ten, my father let me try my hand at steering the boat. I immediately crashed it into someone else's dock.

Every so often, we accepted Dad's plea to try our hand at fishing. He knew we'd catch something if we made even a little bit of effort. When we caught something, he took a Polaroid of us holding up our catch with the camera kept on the boat for just these moments. "Smile, Jenna, and show us the fish!" he'd say proudly.

Given how little I cared for fishing, it surprised even me when, during high school and college summers in Maine, I started waking up early to go fishing with my father and grandfather. When you're a teenager, sleep is the most precious commodity. Yet there I was, rising before the sun was even up. I crept out of bed, slipped into my clothes, and tiptoed past my sleeping sister. I ran down the dewy grass path to the dock, where I met my dad and granddad by the water's edge.

Out there on the boat, in the morning chill, we talked about everything and nothing. Most of the hours we spent just looking out to sea, alone together. No one was there to interrupt us. Politicians spend their days in a constant state of high alert, surrounded by people and noise, so for my dad and granddad, it was a blessing to have a quiet moment outside. I enjoyed having time alone with them, and I especially appreciated being the focus of my Gampy's attention—away from the demands of my other cousins. I also liked the calm feeling I got on the water.

No matter how unsuited I may have been to the sport, the times with my father and grandfather out on the ocean were some of the best of my life. Whenever I caught a fish—entirely by accident or with the help of their seasoned assists—they beamed with pride. They whooped and hollered as if I'd won a marathon. I was happy, but the fish was almost beside the point. I just loved their pride—making them smile and laugh—and feeling the glow of the sun on my face. I always slept well after a day spent in the ocean air.

One sweltering August day in 2004, our family was in Kennebunkport, Maine, for my cousin George's wedding to his girlfriend, Mandy. My father, grandfather, and I took a morning off from family activities to go out on the water in Gampy's boat, the *Fidelity*. How peaceful it was floating in that boat. Then all of a sudden we had company. A boatload of reporters appeared on the horizon.

We were never truly alone on the water. There was the black Coast Guard boat filled with Secret Service, along with the press, who went everywhere with my dad.

My father was president, after all, and everyone knew the wedding was happening that weekend. *I guess I should have brushed my hair,* I thought. I'd been so eager to get out on the water that I'd just thrown my hair up under a green ball cap, put on a white tank top, and grabbed my sunglasses.

Then I felt a tug at the end of my line. A bite! I reeled in and felt another huge pull. This was a big fish! It took all the arm strength I had, but I battled it into the boat.

"Jen!" my father shouted. "Look at that fish! Let's get a picture!"

Then instead of pulling out a Polaroid camera, like the one he used on Rainbo Lake, he said, "Dad! Drive over there!"

Gampy smiled broadly and turned the boat into the wind. In that light and doing his favorite activity, he looked like the nineteen-year-old sailor he once was. As he steered the boat over to the reporters, a hundred cameras flashed, documenting my catch for the country's major newspapers.

"Jenna caught it!" my dad yelled to the reporters. "Jenna caught the fish!"

They got a shot of my thirty-eight-inch striped bass. Then my dad helped me get it off the hook and put it back into the ocean. Unlike the Polaroids, which faded with age or were lost in the course of many moves, this picture of me with the bass ended up on the front page of the *New York Times.*

For the past several years, we haven't fished off the rocky coast of Maine. Our captain, Gampy, was in a wheelchair. I wonder now if maybe my dad spent so much time fishing for the same reason I did—if he, too, was out there for the time alone with his father, in those early mornings when no one cared whether the fish were biting.

From his bedroom window those last few months of his life, Gampy looked out on the rocks where he'd scrambled as a young man and where, as a middle-aged man, he'd taught my father and my cousin Jebby to fly-fish. I know he thought of those happy times and wished he could feel the spray of the sea and the pull of his line once again.

At age seventy-seven, Gampy had a plaque made that read "CAVU: Ceiling and Visibility Unlimited." That was the weather he and his fellow navy pilots always hoped for.

In a letter to his children, he wrote, "I used to seek broad horizons in life and found plenty. Now I don't care if I can't even see Ogunquit. Limited horizons are okay by me just so long as family's in view."

One rainy gray Maine morning, during his last summer on earth, when he was ninety-four, my grandfather looked out on the rocks and saw a fisherman standing there for the first time in years. It was my husband, Henry. He had woken up early that morning with an immediate need to fish. Henry stood in the same spot where generations of Bush men had stood before. As Gampy watched, Henry caught striped bass after striped bass.

When Henry returned to the house after several hours on the rocks, he was soaked through with rain and sea-water.

"I can't believe you stayed out so long!" I said, handing him a towel.

"I did it for Gampy," he said, tears in his eyes.

This past Christmas, with Gampy having passed away, Henry took Mila out on the little bass boat on our ranch in Crawford, Texas, for the first time. She stood proudly next to him with her Fisher-Price rod, casting her line into the murky waters. She looked so much like I did as a little girl—and her interest in fishing was just as tepid as mine had been when I was her age. She was more in-terested in collecting the worms to keep as pets than in catching a fish. Why did she go? For the same reason I did—for time with her dad.

The other night, Poppy asked me, "Mommy, do you think Gampy is in heaven?"

"Yes, of course he is in heaven," I said. The girls have made his passing so bittersweet. These innocent babes of mine: through their unbridled joy and innocence they have helped me walk through the pain of losing someone I loved.

"What do you think it's like in heaven?" she said. "Is it like earth, or is it different?" From the mouth of a three-year-old.

"Well," I told Poppy, "I think in heaven you see the people you love who you've lost. And I think you get to do what you loved most in life."

I can see Gampy now, sitting there in the captain's chair of the *Fidelity*, smiling, holding his fishing rod, letting the ocean take him where it will, ceiling and visibility unlimited.

Henry's Letter to Gampy

Dear Gampy,

Oh, how I wish you had been there.

I woke around 6:30 and instinctively checked the fishing conditions and tides on my phone. I'm really not sure why. I haven't checked it the entire trip. And we like a morning with the girls, enjoying the view and thinking about the day's activities.

Conditions were perfect according to the link that popped up, so I headed out to the fishing shed and put a blue Rapala lure on one of your rods. I went to work on the rocks facing southwest and immediately had a strike on my second cast. Wow! There are fish here. A few casts later I was hooked up and watched twenty fish on the surface around the one I had on! Tons of fish!

A few minutes later I was hooked into a monster

taking line and fishing all directions except home. I saw him go left into the rocks. I had to land this beast but didn't think the odds great. So in my jeans and your fishing jacket (a hall-closet special), I went down into the water and started tiring him out and trying not to break the line. One big wave brought him all the way in. Okay, there's a chance!

Then like millions of waves before, it sucked him right back out. He peeled more line. I thought this was a goner. I kept fishing him, trying to stay calm. He grew tired and I was able to get into the seaweed-laden rocks, now up to my knees in water. Don't fall!

I landed the beast by barrel-hugging him with one arm. His gut was so big I didn't think he'd last long sitting on his side. I was right. I tried to mouth him and was successful quickly. Now get out of the water with everything but don't slip. Three treble hooks can do some serious damage. I got up to semi-dry rock and went to work on releasing the lure. Heart pounding, sweat dripping down my sunglasses, it was an epic battle that I thought you'd appreciate.

Your son snapped a quick photo from the house— doesn't do the fish justice, but the memory will always live large in my mind. I thoroughly enjoyed cleanly releasing that keeper into the seaweed to catch his breath and recover, then eventually head out into the ocean.

The best fishing in Maine has been and will always be Walker's Point.

Love,

Hank

The Opposite of Fear Is Love

The death of a former president dictates a protocol of public mourning. When Gampy died, there were services through the week, culminating in a funeral at the Washington National Cathedral. Several other presidents were in attendance, as were foreign leaders, members of Congress, judges, and many friends.

The morning of Gampy's funeral, I was up at the crack of dawn. My aunt Doro saw that at five A.M. I was already responding on a meditation text chain we share. She called me to see if I was okay. It was typical of her to set aside her own sadness to inquire after others. The truth was, I was struggling, but I knew her heart was broken. At the funeral, I was asked to say a prayer for my grandfather. This is the prayer I read:

A reading from the Book of Revelation:
Then I saw a new heaven and a new earth; for

*the first heaven and the first earth had passed away,
and the sea was no more. And I saw the holy city, the
new Jerusalem, coming down out of heaven from God,
prepared as a bride adorned for her husband. And I
heard a loud voice from the throne saying,*

> "See, the home of God is among mortals.
> He will dwell with them;
> they will be his peoples,
> and God himself will be with them;
> he will wipe every tear from their eyes.
> Death will be no more;
> mourning and crying and pain will be no more,
> for the first things have passed away." . . .

*And the city has no need of sun or moon to shine on
it, for the glory of God is its light, and its lamp is the
Lamb. The nations will walk by its light, and the kings
of the earth will bring their glory into it. Its gates will
never be shut by day—and there will be no night there.*

I cried often that week, but during that service I managed to keep my composure. My grandfather's funeral made me think about the mood of the country that year—the violence, the anger, the images of children suffering on the border—and how I always want to walk on the side of love.

My hero in this quest was a teacher Mila was lucky enough to have for preschool. Maria is one of the most incredible teachers I have ever encountered. She is a light of a human being—a tornado of hugs, smiles, and boundless energy, radiating warmth and goodness. In her tireless, tender way, she makes children feel safe, and she lets parents go off to work sure that their children will not only be taught the building blocks of math and reading but also be taught to love.

In the fall of 2016, I was traveling too often to do drop-offs as regularly as I had for Mila's first year of school. On those mornings when I was out of town, I missed Mila and Poppy, of course, and I also missed seeing Maria.

Ever since I first heard my mother's stories of teaching at Bradfield Elementary School in Dallas, Texas, or JFK in Houston, I have found myself in awe of great teachers. Teaching taught me how difficult it can be to remain calm in the face of chaos, to focus on twenty energetic children at the same time without boring those who are bounding ahead or confusing those who are trailing behind on a particular lesson.

I know that setting your own feelings aside in order to serve the children in your care can require great reserves of strength. When I see a teacher doing all of those things while making it look easy and fun, I take notice.

I couldn't stop thinking about Maria that year for another reason: she is Muslim. The 2016 campaign was dominated by rhetoric that encouraged fear of others.

Barbara was disturbed by the inflammatory language, too. Many members of her global health nonprofit team come from countries around the world, including Muslim countries. She was working hard to help people, and now some of those who were suffering most in the world were being demonized.

Then came election night. Barbara and I have spent many election nights together. Some of these nights we didn't have a personal stake in the outcome, and, obviously, sometimes we did! There were long, endless back-and-forth nights. We have early memories of staying up late, dressed in our American Girl dresses, sitting by our grandfather and our father, feeling the energy in the room shift, wondering why everyone was suddenly sad.

My sister doesn't own a TV, so she came over to my place to watch the election returns that night. Henry was on a trip to Asia for work. It was just Barbara, the girls, and me. Like most everyone, we had read in the newspapers that this election would be a landslide. We planned to have some dinner and watch the results. Then she would go home.

After the girls were tucked snug in their beds, Barbara and I watched the returns. When the winner had not been declared by nine P.M., Barbara ran the four blocks to her apartment to grab pajamas and a pie, returning to spend the night. She and I got into my bed, ate our dessert, and kept the television on until we couldn't keep our eyes open any longer.

The next morning Mila ran into my bedroom to wake

us. At first she was confused. She saw Barbara's long brown hair where her father's head usually is. When she woke us, we turned the TV on and saw a very different result from the one we had been expecting. Barbara and I, sleep-tousled and groggy, looked at each other in surprise.

After we got dressed, I walked Mila to school. It was parent-teacher conference day. As soon as I saw Maria, we reached for each other. To me, Maria represents love. You can hear her singing down the hallway. She beams with a purity of spirit and an inner beauty. Her eyes sparkle. On this day, I thought I saw worry in her expressive eyes.

From the school, I went to a meeting for work. The meeting was, it turned out, made up entirely of women. A TV was on in the background, and we all looked over to see Hillary Clinton giving her concession speech. We watched in silence. Time seemed to stop as together we took in this historic moment.

To all the women, and especially the young women, who put their faith in this campaign and in me, I want you to know that nothing has made me prouder than to be your champion. Now, I know we have still not shattered that highest and hardest glass ceiling, but some day someone will, and hopefully sooner than we might think right now. . . . I believe we are stronger together and we will go forward together. And you should never, ever regret fighting for that. You know, scripture tells us, "Let us not grow weary in doing good, for in due season, we shall reap if we do not lose heart."

In that moment, I was lifted out of the trance I'd been in all day. I remembered that women have the power to lift one another up, to give one another courage. That's what Barbara and I do for each other. She and I decided that very hour to write a book together about what sister-hood looks like in our lives. In that moment, our book, *Sisters First,* was born.

Weeks later, the new administration issued an executive order banning people from coming to the United States from seven mostly Muslim countries. Thinking of Maria and the other friends of mine and of my sister's whom that order targeted, I thought of a speech my father gave in the wake of the September 11 attacks, and I reposted it on Instagram. Here is some of it:

America counts millions of Muslims amongst our citizens, and Muslims make an incredibly valuable contribution to our country. Muslims are doctors, lawyers, law professors, members of the military, en-trepreneurs, shopkeepers, moms and dads. And they need to be treated with respect. . . . Those who feel like they can intimidate our fellow citizens to take out their anger don't represent the best of America, they represent the worst of humankind, and they should be ashamed of that kind of behavior. This is a great country. It's a great country because we share the same values of respect and dignity and human worth.

Some people accused me of taking a political stand by posting that. I disagreed. Loving our neighbor should not be a controversial political stance.

After I posted it, on one morning when I dropped Mila at school, Maria called me into her classroom. She told me she saw the words I had written and said they comforted her. I told her I didn't write them. My father had, years before.

She asked me to thank him, too. She said, "Those words were pure love."

THE SUNDAY AFTER my grandfather's funeral, back in New York, I went to my church, which is nondenominational and close to my apartment. There is no judgment. Everyone is welcome. I don't talk about church often. I've found that it can be awkward to discuss faith. But faith is a big part of my life, and my church is a place of great comfort for me.

Savannah Guthrie attends the same church. Given that I had just lost my grandfather, she suggested we lead the prayers. Together that day we wrote the prayers, ending with my grandfather's prayer on his inauguration day, thirty years earlier. His prayer embodied love over fear, a gentleness of being, and acceptance. He wrote about something we don't talk about enough: how people in power should try to help the weak. To me, that is walking in faith. My grandfather believed, and taught me to believe, too, that the opposite of love is fear.

At church that Sunday, I rose to read and immediately broke down. Something about being in a safe space, surrounded by love, allowed me to let go at last. There were no diplomats' eyes on me, no TV cameras. I couldn't control my sobs. I hadn't broken down in public at all that week. Now I was a puddle. I cry often, but this was different. I could barely breathe.

This is what I read, through sobs, Savannah holding my shaking hand:

I

Dearest Lord Jesus,

We pray to you. We approach you with hearts open, hearts tender, hearts hurting.

Today, Lord, we thank you that weeping lasts for a night but joy comes in the morning.

Rejoicing comes in the morning. Hope comes in the morning.

Thank you for being the god of joy. The god who wipes every tear, not just for a moment, but for eternity. We thank you, God, for the "new heaven and new earth" that the prophets saw all those millennia ago.

We rejoice in the god who reunites lost loves. Who bandages wounds. Who tends to broken hearts. Who makes right what was wrong and could never be fixed. Whose plan is a final, all-encompassing answer to brokenness, to hurt, to death itself. We pray to the Lord who triumphs, then gives us the victory.

We pray with joy because our Lord has the last word. Because this earth cannot contain your heaven. We pray in anticipation and expectation of the eternal joy that awaits us.

Lord, in your mercy, hear our prayer.

II

We pray to you, Lord.

For hope and humility over despair and arrogance.

We pray for those we have lost—all the while knowing they have entered the forever embrace of their god and now light up the heavens like a thousand points of light.

We thank you, Lord, for the power of a quiet example. We thank you, Lord, that in your kingdom, the last will be first; the kind and gentle ones will inherit the earth. Thank you, Lord, that your way is not the world's way. It is not the loud way, not the self-serving way, not the way that grabs everything for itself but instead gives everything of itself.

Lord, touch us this morning with renewed hope and joy as only you can. Help us to give thanks in all circumstances, for this is your plan for us and your gift to us.

Lord, in your mercy, hear our prayer.

III

[Savannah read this one while I tried to pull myself together.]

We pray for those for whom joy seems impossible. Whose bodies ache, whose spirits fail, whose thirst is not quenched and whose bellies burn with hunger. We pray for those born seemingly without even a chance. But, Lord, you know different. So come to them, Lord. Save them. Make yourself known. Fill their needs and fill their hearts.

We pray with gratitude to you, Lord, for you came to rescue us, you came to set us free—presently and eternally. Free from earthly pains that cripple us, earthly chains that confine us, earthly limitations that tether us—Lord, let gravity's pull that binds us to this lost world finally be broken. We pray for lightness, for release, for freedom, for eternal homecoming. For your "glorious and inexpressible joy."

Lord, in your mercy, hear our prayer.

IV

And finally a prayer said on a January morning in Washington almost thirty years ago.

Heavenly Father, we bow our heads and thank you for your love.

Make us strong to do your work, willing to heed and hear your will and write on our heart these words: use power to help people.

For we are given power not to advance our own purposes, nor to make a great show in the world, nor a name.

There is but one just use of power and it is to serve people.

Help us remember, Lord, amen.

Lord, in your mercy, hear our prayer.

I sat back down, my face puffy, and looked over at Henry. "I'm embarrassed," I said. "I lost it."

"Hey," Henry whispered, "at least it wasn't at the National Cathedral."

I laughed. That was just the kind of dry joke my grandparents would have made. They were always making cracks like that, then holding hands and laughing uproariously. Looking around the church, at my community and my family and my friends, I thought once again how even on the darkest days God will show us cause for joy.

Times I Have Cried (a Partial List)

- At kids' birthday parties, while watching my daughters dance with abandon.
- Walking down the aisle to marry Henry.
- When Poppy met Gampy, her namesake, for the first time.
- At parent-teacher conferences, when I hear glowing reports.
- When the Oak Ridge Boys played at my Gampy's funeral.
- At all Kleenex commercials (ironic, I know).
- Watching proudly as my dad was sworn in as president.
- Often as I've written this book—both happy tears of joy and cleansing tears of grief.
- When my grandfather read love letters he wrote to my grandmother during World War II on the *Today* show. He cried as he read, which created a chain

reaction. By the end of the interview, I had tears flowing down my face, mascara everywhere. My steely-eyed grandmother later teased us, saying we were "two John Boehners" (Boehner was a famous crybaby. I relate, John).

- While conducting many interviews for work, listening to people open their hearts. (Sometimes I cry when those I'm interviewing do not. I call this the reverse Barbara Walters.)

- In a motorcade with my Ganny when she came to visit Dallas with Millie, her springer spaniel, in tow. In the car, I finished the chapter book *A Dog Called Kitty*. I wept uncontrollably when (spoiler alert) the protagonist—a dog named Kitty—dies. As we drove, my Ganny waved out the window. Texans were surprised to see, out of nowhere, the smiling First Lady and her bawling school-age granddaughter. Ganny finally gestured out the window, saying to me, "They're going to think I'm beating you!" I tried to smile and wave to the crowds, but I continued to whimper while I did it.

- Listening to music, especially songs like Bette Midler's "Wind Beneath My Wings." Tell me you can keep it together while watching the movie *Beaches*. Barbara and I wept side by side when we watched it as girls.

- Six months pregnant with Poppy, hormones ablaze, in front of hundreds of people. As I waited to give a speech onstage, the moderator read my bio: "Jenna married Henry Hager in 2008. In 2013, they had a daughter, Margaret Laura Hager. . . ." The second I heard her name, I burst into tears. I thought, *That's right! I* am *the mother of Mila Hager!* The room was mostly filled with men, who were clearly alarmed by my sobbing. I heard them murmuring, "What is this? What is happening? Is she okay? What do we do?" I pulled myself together and wiped the tears away. I gave my talk. And I refused to feel ashamed by my tears. I thought of my grandfather, after whom I would name this new baby growing within me, and I thought, *Gampy would understand.* It was one of the guiding rules of his life: "Don't be afraid to shed a tear." I think about that rule, and therefore about him, every time I cry. In other words, I think about him all the time.

Gentle Protection

When I was a little girl, we lived on West Golf Course Road in Midland, Texas, near my mother's parents, my Pa and Grammee. Midland was a small town where nothing exciting ever happened. The town gossips had to content themselves with scandals involving tumbleweeds and dust tornadoes. But one day when Barbara and I were four years old, something incredible happened—in our own backyard.

Barbara and I were in the house playing hospital with a stuffed bear when out the window we saw a man cut through our backyard. The man was fleeing the police! The cops followed hot on his trail. To escape, the crook jumped over our fence. In the process, he tore his jeans and injured his leg.

The sight of the robber's blood spattered on our wooden fence remains one of my earliest and, to this day, most vibrant recollections. It's as clear a memory of something that took place thirty-four years ago can be, vivid to this day because it was by far the most dramatic thing that had ever happened to me (and I was a little girl dreaming of the dramatic!).

Barbara and I ran screaming to find our mother. In both of our memories of the event, at the time of the incident our mom was lounging in the tub. (Like many Baby Boomer parents, she did not helicopter!) She jumped out of the bath, threw on clothes, and called our father at work to tell him to come home immediately.

Soon our father and more police arrived. Having our dad at home, we could once again exhale. If he was around, we felt protected, and we saw by the way the police talked to him that they, too, respected his quiet authority. They even asked him to help them canvass the neighborhood, looking for the criminal. Our dad—the superhero!

To ensure we wouldn't miss a thing, we stayed close the entire time the police were in our home. One of the policemen, while walking through the doorway out to the stone patio, patted little Barbara on the head and said, "Excuse me, little lady."

"He said that like you're a grown-up!" I marveled, envy dripping from my voice.

We remember every detail of that day, but the feeling Barbara and I recall most intensely is that reassurance our father gave us. When he was there, we felt safe.

The downside was that when he wasn't there, I pined for him. The first time my parents traveled internationally without my sister and me, it was to Gambia; we were about nine years old. Pa and Grammee stayed with us, and for part of the time so did our first grade teacher (who bought us a BarNone and a Slurpee after school, something our mom never did). I was surrounded by loving, responsible adults. It didn't matter. I lay distraught in my parents' bed, imagining their deaths by flash flood, rhino stampede, and malaria. I fell asleep clutching a framed photograph of them. (As has already been established, I was slightly dramatic.)

The sense of safety we felt when we were close to our dad carried into our teenage years. Whenever Barbara and I got our hearts broken, he told us we could do better. And, more than anything else, he listened to us talk, asking questions and offering sympathetic insights. His protection was gentle—nothing like the stereotype you see of overprotective Texas fathers standing at the door waiting with a shotgun!

Once when I was fifteen my boyfriend and I were on the phone arguing late into the night. The house was dark. My parents and sister were sleeping. Finally my father, who had woken up and overheard enough of the commotion, walked in and said to me, "It's time to go to bed."

"Well, will you tell *Blake* it's time to go to bed?" I said in a huff.

I'd said it rhetorically, but my father came over and calmly took the phone out of my hand. Into the receiver he said, "Blake, man, it's time to go to bed. Don't call back again tonight. You can talk tomorrow, okay? Good night."

He hung up the phone, kissed my forehead, and turned out the light.

His intervention was so simple and efficient that as I lay there in the dark, I failed to remember what Blake and I were even fighting about; my father had ended it. I fell soundly asleep.

A couple of months later, when Blake decided at the last minute to disinvite me as his senior prom date, I cried from embarrassment and disappointment, and because, as a sophomore, I now wouldn't get to wear my beautiful prom dress for who knew how long. "Go ahead and wear the dress now!" my father suggested.

He put on music, and when I emerged from my room in the dress, he danced me around the living room. It didn't completely cure my teenage despair, but it did feel good to twirl in that dress and to laugh. And in retrospect it was a more memorable night than I was likely to have had at the prom.

IN THE MONTHS after September 11, Barbara and I had that same feeling of safety, knowing our father was leading our country. In public, he sometimes came across as having a bit of a swagger. When he said things like "We won't let a thug bring this country down," I was surprised, because at home he never spoke like that. (Our mother later told him she didn't approve of the word *thug,* and he stopped using it.)

He was portrayed in public, we knew, as not particularly

scholarly. At the 2005 White House Correspondents' Association Dinner, he said, "I look forward to these dinners where I'm supposed to be funny . . . intentionally." But we knew him as an avid reader, especially of history. His favorite books were biographies of other presidents and world leaders. He believed they helped keep him focused on the job at hand. Whenever people said in private conversations, "You've had it so tough!" as in the wake of the terror attacks, he offered counterexamples from the past: "What about Lincoln during the war? Look at FDR's second term. I can't imagine how it felt to be Washington . . ."

He believed that they had it harder—especially, he said, because he had certain advantages that many great men did not. One was the gift, he said, of being married to my mom, whose preternaturally calm nature gave him strength. He has since reflected that because he knew she was taking such good care of Barbara and me he was able to do his work without worrying about us.

While my father was president, there was a vast difference between our dad, the gentle protector, and the way we saw him depicted on TV. But I understood; it was impossible for strangers to know the dad I knew. In the public eye, you're a two-dimensional character. Watching a *Saturday Night Live* parody, I searched for the real man, the one I knew. He wasn't there. Of course not. No one else was there to witness him comfort me on prom night, or speed home from work in Midland, or accept our librarian mother's wise counsel on word choice. Barbara and I understood, too, that in the wake of September 11 our father had to project power and decisiveness in a way that made Americans feel safe and that people around the world could understand. That was a terrible and terrifying time, and he did his best to lead us all through it.

IN THE SUMMER of 2002, I was living in D.C., working at a charter school, and I invited some girlfriends from college to Camp David for a visit. My mother was away on a hiking trip. The first evening, we had dinner together with my dad and then watched a movie. My father went to bed, and my friends and I stayed up late talking in our cabin. The next morning, very early, my dad rushed into our cabin. He had been up for hours but we were still asleep.

"Wake up, girls," he said, adding to me, "Put on your glasses. There's a plane flying overhead. The Secret Service needs to move us all right now. Quickly now, follow me."

Instantly alert, we leaped up and followed him.

I couldn't find my glasses, so he guided me across the way to a bunker under one of the other cabins—just as he had led my mom and their dog Barney, while carrying their cat Willard, following an alarm in the middle of the night on September 11. Now, in 2002, my friends and I sat there in the bunker, shivering in our pajamas, as our father reassured us. "It's probably just a passenger jet in a no-fly zone," he said. "Don't worry." (It would turn out that his guess was right.)

I nodded, not telling him what was on my mind—that I wasn't worried because he was next to me.

AT MY GRANDFATHER'S funeral in 2018, my father's presence soothed me yet again. Sitting in a pew of the National Cathedral, a place with such a storied history, I grew nervous knowing that I needed to walk up the stone steps to read a passage in front of more than 1,500 people, a number of powerful world leaders among them, in addition to all those at home watching on television. I would be speaking from the same pulpit from which my father spoke to the nation just three days after September 11.

On that day, he'd told the country,

We are here in the middle hour of our grief. So many have suffered so great a loss, and today we express our nation's sorrow. . . .

God's signs are not always the ones we look for. We learn in tragedy that his purposes are not always our own.

Yet the prayers and private suffering, whether in our homes or in this great cathedral, are known and heard and understood. There are prayers that help us last through the day or endure the night. There are prayers of friends and strangers that give us strength for the journey. And there are prayers that yield our will to a will greater than our own. . . .

*In every generation, the world has produced ene-
mies of human freedom. They have attacked America
because we are freedom's home and defender. And the
commitment of our fathers is now the calling of our
time.*

While giving that powerful speech, he did not look at
his parents or his wife in the front row. He knew that if
he did he would break down—and he believed that the
last thing the nation needed in that moment was a sobbing president.

When my father returned to the pew after his speech,
he continued to avoid the gaze of his family, but his father reached over and took his hand and held it for a
second. My father looked back at his father, and they exchanged a glance of respect and resolve. My grandfather
had traded seats with Bill Clinton, breaking with the traditional diplomatic order, so he could sit closer to his
son. My Gampy, our father's gentle protector, was more
than an ex-president in that moment; he was a father
comforting his son.

I can barely look at photographs of that moment without tearing up.

Now it was my turn to speak at the National Cathedral. I made my way down the aisle to the podium. As I
passed the pew where he sat, my father whispered, "Go
get 'em, Jen."

When I walked back up the aisle a few minutes later,
having kept my composure even while gently touching

my grandfather's casket, my father reached out and held my hand, just as his father had held his in this same place seventeen years earlier.

And to me that's what my dad's calm protection, which he inherited from his father, looks like: a hand holding yours while you cry, a voice telling you it's time for bed because he can hear the fatigue in your words, a steady hand guiding you to a bunker, saying it will all be okay. When my babies were born, I loved passing them into his strong arms. He held them the way he'd held us— the way, emotionally, he still does. It has been a disappointment to me that the world didn't always see the side of him that we did, but I'm grateful beyond measure that I do.

A Letter from Jenna and Barbara to Sasha and Malia

Dear Sasha and Malia,

We were seven when our beloved grandfather was sworn in as the 41st President of the United States. We stood proudly on the platform, our tiny hands icicles, as we lived history. We listened intently to the words spoken on Inauguration Day about service, duty, honor. But, being seven, we didn't quite understand the gravity of the position our grandfather was committing to. We watched as the bands marched by—the red, white, and blue streamers welcoming us to a new role: the family members of a president.

We also first saw the White House through the innocent, optimistic eyes of children. We stood on the North Lawn gazing with wonder at her grand portico. The White House was alive with devoted and loving people, many of whom had worked in her halls for decades. Three of the White House ushers, Buddy, Ramsey, and "Smiley," greeted us when we stepped into her intimidating hallway. Their laughter and embraces made us feel welcome right away. Sasha and Malia, here is some advice to you from two sisters who have stood where you will stand and who have lived where you will live:

- Surround yourself with loyal friends. They'll protect and calm you and join in on some of the fun, and appreciate the history.
- If you're traveling with your parents over Halloween, don't let it stop you from doing what you would normally do. Dress up in some imaginative, elaborate costume (if you are like us, a pack of Juicy Fruit and a vampiress) and trick-or-treat down the plane aisle.
- If you ever need a hug, go find Ramsey. If you want to talk football, look for Buddy. And, if you just need a smile, look for "Smiley."
- And, a note on White House puppies—our sweet puppy Spot was nursed on the lawn of the White House. And then of course, there's Barney, who most recently bit a reporter. Cherish your animals because sometimes you'll need the quiet comfort that only animals can provide.
- Slide down the banister of the solarium, go to T-ball games, have swimming parties, and play

Sardines on the White House lawn. Have fun and enjoy your childhood in such a magical place to live and play.

- When your dad throws out the first pitch for the Yankees, go to the game.
- In fact, go to anything and everything you possibly can: the Kennedy Center for theater, State dinners, Christmas parties (the White House staff party is our favorite!), museum openings, arrival ceremonies, and walks around the monuments. Just go. Four years goes by so fast, so absorb it all, enjoy it all!

For four years, we spent our childhood holidays and vacations in the historic house. We could almost feel the presence of all the great men and women who had lived here before us. When we played house, we sat behind the east sitting room's massive curtains as the light poured in, illuminating her yellow walls. Our seven-year-old imaginations soared as we played in the enormous, beautiful rooms; our dreams, our games, as romantic as her surroundings. At night, the house sang us quiet songs through the chimneys as we fell asleep.

In late December, when snow blanketed the front lawn, all of our cousins overtook the White House. Thirteen children between the ages of two and twelve ran throughout her halls, energized by the crispness in the air and the spirit of the season.

Every room smelled of pine; the entire house was adorned with thistle; garlands wound around every banister. We sat on her grand staircase and spied on the holiday dancing below. Hours were spent playing hide-and-go-seek. We used a stage in the grand ballroom to produce a play about Santa and his reindeer. We watched as the national Christmas tree was lit and admired the chef as he put the final icing on the gingerbread house.

When it was time, we left the White House. We said our goodbyes to her and to Washington. We weren't sure if we would spend time among her historical walls again, or ever walk the National Mall, admiring the cherry blossoms that resembled puffs of cotton candy. But we did return. This time we were eighteen. The White House welcomed us back, and there is no doubt that it is a magical place at any age.

As older girls, we were constantly inspired by the amazing people we met, politicians and great philosophers like Vaclav Havel. We dined with royalty, heads of state, authors, and activists. We even met the queen of England and managed to see the Texas Longhorns after they won the national championship. We traveled with our parents to foreign lands and were deeply moved by what we saw. Trips to Africa inspired and motivated us to begin working for HIV/AIDS relief and for the rights of women and children all over the world.

Now, the White House ballrooms were filled with energy and music as we danced. The east sitting room became a peaceful place to read and study. We ran on the track in the front lawn, and squared off in sisterly bowling duels down in the basement alley.

This Christmas, with the enchanting smell of the holidays encompassing her halls, we will again be saying our goodbyes to the White House. Sasha and Malia, it is your turn now to fill the White House with laughter.

And finally, although it's an honor and full of so many extraordinary opportunities, it isn't always easy being a member of the club you are about to join. Our dad, like yours, is a man of great integrity and love, a man who always put us first. We still see him now as we did when we were seven: as our loving daddy. Our dad, who read to us nightly, taught us how to score baseball games. He is our father, not the sketch in a paper or part of a skit on TV. Many people will think they know him, but they have no idea how he felt the day you were born, the pride he felt on your first day of school, or how much you both love being his daughters. So here is our most important piece of advice: remember who your dad really is.

"To Thine Own Self Be True"

One of the most precious videos I have is from the first trip baby Mila took to meet her great-grandparents in Maine. A video camera recorded the moment when she was first placed in my Gampy's arms. I've watched the scene many times.

As we sat for drinks on floral couches in the living room of the house I'd visited every year of my life, Gampy crooned to Mila, "When you walk through a cloud, keep your head held high!"

She gazed up at him, rapt.

Struck by the contrast between this man who had lived such a full life and this precious infant, a mere three months old, who couldn't yet speak and had her whole life ahead of her, I felt called to ask a question. Pointing at Mila, I said, "Gampy, when you see a baby just starting her life, like that one, what would you say are the most important things that you've learned over your life?"

He thought for a second. Then he looked at her with affection and said in a strong, quiet voice, "Be true to yourself. To thine own self be true."

That line from *Hamlet,* while spoken by Polonius as part of a comic monologue, rings true to me as a reminder to cultivate self-acceptance. That is something I and many women I know have struggled with at various points—for me, it was a particular challenge in middle school.

When I was in seventh grade, like so many middle school girls, I didn't love seeing my body in a bathing suit. A large, irregularly shaped birthmark on my thigh made the prospect of swimwear even more daunting. When walking around pools, I tried to hold my hand in such a way as to cover it up. I must not have done a very good job, though, because after my then-boyfriend Eric and I went swimming with a group of friends, he broke up with me, citing the unsightly birthmark as his reason.

Right around that time when I felt the most terrible about myself, TV cameras arrived in my family's home. My dad was running for governor, so a local news reporter came over to interview us.

I would have been thrilled to see the cameras if I hadn't just experienced a breakup. With dreams of being a Broadway star filling my head, I incessantly sang "Castle on a Cloud," always with a broom in hand. When I'd first heard about this TV appearance I imagined it might be my big break. *Les Miz* casting directors sitting at home would notice the chubby middle schooler and shout, "There's our Cosette!"

Now I just hoped to make it through the interview without humiliating myself. The task seemed simple enough. The segment was a straightforward profile of the politician and his family. By beaming at my dad and answering questions about our lives, we would help people see him as the lovable family man we knew him to be.

Sitting on the couch, we were doing a good job until, all of a sudden, we were interrupted by the ringing of a phone. It was Barbara's and my private line, which had been recently installed as a Christmas gift, to our great delight.

My father said, in front of everyone, "Oh, is that *Eric* calling?"

That was my dad being himself—disregarding the cameramen, sound guys, and local reporter in her trim suit, to joke with his daughter about her boyfriend. Now, at the height of my awkward stage, clear braces and all, I did not appreciate his attempt at levity.

I hadn't told him that Eric had dumped me that week, but he must have known as soon as he saw my face, for it instantly turned a deep red.

The cameras kept rolling.

I hurried to get the phone, so discomfited that on the way I ran directly into a wall. (I've always been a klutz—

less Most Likely to Succeed than Most Likely to Trip Crossing the Stage at Graduation.)

You'd think the news station editors would take pity on a young girl having a bad day, a girl who clearly longed to be flawless like teenage actors on TV, with their straight teeth, unblemished skin, and uncanny sense of how to get through a doorway. But no. My accident aired on the evening news. I suppose they thought it made us seem like a real family. *See? Even politicians have mortified, uncoordinated adolescent daughters!*

That was not the last time I would be embarrassed on television or in the press. I have misspoken. I have had bad hair. I have gone blank. All in front of millions of people. And I have heard about it. Everyone from op-ed writers to trolls on Twitter have parsed my words and my appearance. I've been on the covers of tabloids with my sister alongside headlines like "Oops! They Did It Again: The Bush Girls' Latest Scrape."

I'd like to say it's never bothered me, but the truth is that negative comments have sometimes hurt me more than they should. Why can we read twenty complimentary things without absorbing their kindness, whereas one snide attack can stop us cold?

I think it's because the comment we remember is always one that gets to the heart of the thing that we worry about most. As a tween, I was preoccupied with how I looked. When Eric broke up with me, it confirmed a fear of mine that my birthmark made me unattractive, unlovable. And I never have fully outgrown that insecurity. I still find myself, now in my late thirties, reaching for a sarong to cover up my birthmark when I go swimming with my girls.

And I have other, bigger fears now. One is that people will judge me either positively or negatively because of my family. I worry that people who take issue with my father's policies will believe he and I agree on everything politically or that I have to answer for his decisions. I worry, too, that people who love the Bush family will be extra nice to me or provide me with opportunities only because of my bloodline.

When I got my job at *Today,* I received thousands of notes of congratulations from friends and family and viewers. But for some reason one tweet that said I got the job only because of my dad was the one that I reflected on most that first week. It resonated with my most vulnerable part, corroborating an inner voice that said, *That person is right. You're not good enough on your own.* That comment hung over me like a dark cloud when I should have been enjoying my new job.

One day I was sitting side by side in the hair and makeup room at the *Today* show with Maria Shriver, the Emmy-winning journalist and former First Lady of California. Her friendship is valuable to me for many reasons, but especially because she offers a wise perspective on what it can mean to come from a political family.

As we had our makeup done, Maria asked me what

was new. I began talking through my schedule. It was an insane blur of travel and work. Maria stopped me and said, "I'd like to tell you a story."

She told me that she had just gone through security at the airport when a TSA agent had called out, "Hey! Aren't you a Kennedy?" (She is the niece of John F. Kennedy and Robert F. Kennedy.)

"Now, I'm a sixtyish-year-old woman," Maria said. "I've been a journalist for decades. I've won awards. I've raised huge sums of money for Alzheimer's research. And for some people, none of that will ever matter. I will always be known as a Kennedy. That's also true for you. No matter what you do, you will always be known as a Bush."

I knew she spoke the truth. Like Maria, I've worked myself to the bone to distinguish myself from my family, to prove that I'm worthy of my job and my life. My sister and I both do. I've come to realize we work so hard because we don't want to be accused of nepotism or to give any support to people who say success has been handed to us.

Maria forced me to ask myself: *Why so much work? What truly fills me up?* I love my job, but I also needed to stop and think about why I was working such long hours. Perhaps because it feels easier to wage a fight against real and imagined critics than to do what my grandfather said is the most important thing: be true to yourself, know who you are, and be at peace.

When people ask, "How can you bear being on TV and being constantly criticized for every little thing?" I say that my skin has become thickened by decades of public life. I've come to realize that in my heart I know what is true and what is not. I can't let strangers make me doubt myself or see me as someone who I'm not.

Whenever I hear people say something about me that I know to be false, I watch that video of my Gampy telling tiny baby Mila, "To thine own self be true." I watch her eyes in the video, looking up at him with wonder. From those very first moments, she trusted him completely. And I believe she heard his message. Now, six years later, she is completely and unapologetically herself. I find myself studying that tape, letting the two of them teach me what it looks like to feel free.

Comfort Care

A hint of warmth one Sunday in an otherwise bleak April brought me to the park with my girls. The hours passed in a whirl of snacks and slides until, in what felt like no time at all, the setting sun began to cast long shadows across the blacktop. A chill in the air made me realize for the hundredth time that I had failed—once again the girls were not dressed warmly enough. With the sun going down, soon they would be shivering. It was time to go home.

As I gathered the scooter and stroller, the wipes and the leftover Pirate's Booty, I glanced at my phone for the first time since our arrival. My heart sank. I had more than fifty texts. From experience, I knew that so many messages could mean only bad news.

As I navigated our way home, I anxiously skimmed through the messages. Many of the texts were from colleagues. The first one—simply I'm so sorry—stopped me abruptly in my tracks on a Manhattan sidewalk. Mila slammed into me on her scooter.

I made sure Mila was okay and then read the text again:
I'm so sorry . . .

Why was she sorry? What had happened?

Another message mentioned praying for my grandmother.

Had Ganny passed away?

As I pushed Poppy's stroller and Mila scooted along, I continued to scroll and slowly realized that no one was dead. Ganny had merely made a public announcement. In the face of new health problems, she would receive only "comfort care" going forward.

I was relieved that she was still alive. And yet I was confused by the wording of this statement. What did *comfort care* mean? Why had she made this announcement? Would we lose her soon?

When I arrived home, I turned on a cartoon for the girls and called my parents. My mother answered on the first ring. I said I was sorry I hadn't seen her texts earlier. Then I asked her what *comfort care* meant.

"Comfort care means Ganny does not want any more extreme treatments to cure her," my mother explained. "She will have pain relief, but nothing more."

"Does this mean she's dying?" I asked.

"There is no way to know," my mom said. "But I would call her to say goodbye."

More than once, I have looked at my grandmother and thought, *This woman is invincible.* The epitome of strength, Ganny always seemed like she could conquer anything. Several times when my grandfather was thought to be at death's door, she said he would recover, and almost as if he didn't want to disobey her, he got better. I knew she wouldn't live forever, but I couldn't imagine life without her.

My parents had just recently spent time with her and had said their goodbyes. Henry would be in Texas the next day for business and was going to try to see her. I wanted to hop on a plane that very minute to join them, but I needed to work the next morning. I booked a flight that would leave on Tuesday, the day after a long-planned segment for the *Today* show aired.

That night Barbara came to my apartment. We searched each other's eyes for some reassurance that this was not the end. We stood at my kitchen counter and decided to call our Ganny.

As the phone rang, we imagined our grandmother bedridden, assuming a nurse or relative would answer in a hushed tone. Instead, Ganny answered the phone herself. "Hi, girls!" she said in what seemed to us to be her usual strong voice.

"We love you so much!" I said. "You're the best grandmother in the world. How do you feel?"

My voice cracked. Tears sprang to my eyes. *What if this is the last time we talk to this force of nature?* I thought.

Twins often cry in unison; our histories and our sensibilities are inextricably linked. Barbara started weeping seconds after I did. We tried to hide the pain in our voices, but our Ganny heard us.

"Girls, don't worry!" she said with a laugh. "They're

making it sound like I'm already dead. Don't believe everything you read."

That was our Ganny. She was dying and her reaction was to comfort us—and using one of her favorite phrases. She'd spoken those same words many times over the years whenever she read something critical about someone she loved. She had used them to defend Barbara and me in our youth from accusations that we were too wild. To people who criticized us for underage drinking, for example, Ganny said they should mind their own business and not believe everything they read—we were good kids. Ganny had a reputation as an enforcer, but there were lines she would not cross. She was hesitant to give my mother advice because she didn't want to come across as the typical domineering mother-in-law, and she gave us the space we needed to make mistakes when we were young.

Before we hung up, Ganny told us that her best friend had been there just the day before for a visit. They'd had a lovely time gossiping and sipping cocktails. This did not sound to me like a woman on the cusp of death. That night, I slept well.

THE NEXT MORNING, a Monday, I woke up with a bad sore throat. I went out to the horse farm in New Jersey that was the subject of my report. We were kicking off National Volunteer Appreciation Week, and I felt an obligation to be there to call attention to this impressive nonprofit.

While I stood waiting for my live shot outside a barn, Savannah Guthrie and Hoda Kotb called me on air to ask me how my Ganny was doing and to send love.

"Thanks, guys," I replied. "We are grateful for her. She is the best grandma anyone could have ever had—or *have*." I felt a rush of embarrassment for having just spoken of her in the past tense, but I forged ahead. "And Barbara and I talked to her last night. She's in great spirits and she's a fighter. She's an enforcer. She reminded me not to believe everything you read. So we're grateful for her and for everybody's prayers and thoughts. And just know the world is better because she is in it."

They warmly said they did know that, and they asked me how my grandfather and mom and dad were holding up.

"She's with my grandpa, the man she's loved for over seventy-three years," I said. "They are surrounded by family. The fact that we're together in this and he still says, 'I love you, Barbie,' every night is pretty remarkable."

As I signed off, I winced. I couldn't believe that I had slipped into the past tense. Our Ganny was still here, surrounded by loved ones . . . and here I was speaking of her in a tense of goodbyes, memories, and heartbreak. I quickly collected myself, but the slip hurt every time I recalled it.

I still had to go live for my segment. I moved inside

the barn, where I petted a horse while I listened to the programming that was leading into my package. One of the headlines that I heard made me tear up, even though I knew it was coming: "Barbara Bush will seek comfort care."

The freezing early-morning air felt like daggers in my throat, and hearing that phrase made me shiver: *comfort care*. Why could I still not get my head around what that meant? Perhaps because it was a term I did not associate with my grandmother. Our Ganny was not a traditional comforter. She did not coddle. She spoke bluntly, sometimes harshly. And yet, as I thought about it, having her in the world was always a comfort. Knowing she was there—to set boundaries, to keep us all in line, to tell it like it is—had always made me feel hopeful. She made everyone in the family better. Without her, who would be there to keep order, to make sure everyone lived up to their potential, to remind us to behave?

The camera light came on and Hoda threw to me. I tried to quickly shake off my thoughts and to be present, though I could see in the monitor that I looked a little like a deer in headlights. "Hey, guys! I'm at Sunnyside Equestrian Center," I said, trying to sound cheerful and hoping I was at least making sense. Try as I might, my mind was still with my grandmother. "Kids facing challenges of all kinds come here to work with therapeutic horses like this one and an army of volunteers! They're changing lives one amazing horseback ride at a time!" I put the stress on strange syllables. I pronounced *equestrian* as if it were in a foreign language. I hoped no one would notice that I was just trying not to cry.

"Back to you," I told the studio. "We're all in tears." By now my throat was burning and my voice was a painful-sounding squeak.

In the studio, my colleagues clapped and said, "Bravo!"

I was glad to have made it through, but I could not wait to pack up so I could fly to Texas.

ON TUESDAY, I woke up feeling horrible, but I called my parents and told them I was heading to Houston.

"What's going on with your voice?" my father asked.

"Nothing," I choked out. "Just a sore throat."

"Didn't Mila have strep a couple of weeks ago?" he asked.

She had.

"You should get a strep test before you fly," he said. "Gampy is there, along with others. You can't get them sick."

I got a test and it turned out he was right—I did have strep. I started on antibiotics, knowing I couldn't fly until the following day, when they'd have kicked in.

While I waited for the drugs to take effect, I received a call. My grandmother had just passed away.

I was in shock. She had been so present just two days earlier. Now she was gone. It felt symbolic to me that by this point I could barely croak out a single word. Ganny's voice was so strong. With her departure, it seemed that my voice, too, had faded.

Henry called to see how I was and to say he was on his way to my parents' place in Dallas. I told him that Mila had handled the news as she often does—by drawing pictures. Her hand-eye coordination was still developing, but her tiny hands created a dozen stick figures of her Great-Ganny. When she handed them to me, she said, "See? Now we'll always remember what she looked like." I also tried to prepare him for the scene he was likely to walk into when he arrived at my parents' house.

"Everyone is going to be really sad," I said. "When you get there, you should probably just put your head down and go to bed."

He said he would do that and call me later.

I hung up feeling sorry for myself. He was going to be wrapped in the warm embrace of a full house in mourning while I lay alone in our bed, throat burning, watching the news on TV.

Later that night, I was getting myself ready for bed and half watching the news when the phone rang. It was Henry calling again. On FaceTime, I saw that he looked rosy-cheeked. He told me that I'd been far off the mark when I'd warned him that he would find a somber scene.

When he arrived, Henry encountered an amiable John Boehner, smoking, and a few glasses of red wine into the evening. My parents do not drink, but tipsy Boehner had lifted the mood of the room. He made it feel like an Irish wake. He even wound up telling Henry all about his new investments in marijuana businesses. Henry was enthusiastically recalling their conversation about the edibles market before I cut him off.

"Could you perhaps have found a better day to discuss pot legalization with John Boehner?" I said. I tried to sound stern, but a smile crept in around my scowl. I actually found it quite hilarious, and I suspected my grandmother would have appreciated the humor, too.

After all, in her last phone call with my father, he had said, "I love you, Mom. You've been a fabulous mother."

"I love you, too," she'd replied. "You're my favorite son . . . on the phone."

OUR GANNY DIED the way she lived: on her own terms. She was unapologetically herself up to the very end, and I secretly loved that she was able to hear people's warmest memories of her life. In her final days, the presidential biographer Jon Meacham called and asked if she'd like to hear her eulogy, which he had written in advance. She said yes. His tribute included a story about how he'd complained to her about being mistaken for the author John Grisham. He expected grandmotherly consolation. Instead, she'd replied, "Well, how do you think poor John Grisham would feel? He's a very handsome man."

She told Meacham she approved of the eulogy.

Some rules are spoken or typed to hang on the backs of doors; others are taught quietly and by example. Our culture fears death in so many ways. And yet, in her maverick style, Ganny did not fear dying. She would accept only comfort care because she wanted to die as she lived—surrounded by those she loved, master of her own domain. Did she know that by dying fearlessly she was showing us the way and teaching us one last great lesson?

I smile to think of her in her final days: lying in bed in Houston, watching shows about her life, feeling grateful—and also disagreeing with the pundits! Watching the news about her legacy in those days before her death, she was able to essentially witness her own funeral. That, too, was classically Ganny. She didn't like to miss a thing.

She died in her own bed, holding my grandpa's hand. Her funeral four days later, held at St. Martin's Episcopal Church in Houston, where she had attended services for fifty years, was serious but also warm. There were jokes. My uncle Jeb said, "She called her style a benevolent dictatorship, but honestly it wasn't always benevolent." We all laughed knowingly.

Between the viewing and funeral, some eight thousand people came to say goodbye to her, including four of the five living former presidents (Jimmy Carter was overseas). Melania Trump sat alongside the Clintons and the Obamas. The choir sang "My Country 'Tis of Thee."

Eight of Ganny's grandsons—my cousins—carried her coffin out of St. Martin's after the service. Gampy's wheelchair, pushed by my father, followed behind the casket. Mourners stood all along the motorcade route. Some wore fake pearls in her honor. She would have loved it.

Ganny was buried at the George H.W. Bush Presidential Library and Museum in a grave next to Robin, the daughter Ganny and Gampy lost to leukemia at the age of three. She was famous in the family for saying, often, "I love you more than tongue can tell." Standing there looking at the two stones side by side, I felt a sense of peace. I imagined them reunited. My daydream was given expression by Marshall Ramsey, a *Clarion-Ledger* cartoonist. Soon after her death, he published a cartoon that showed Ganny arriving at the gates of heaven. The first thing she sees is her long-lost blond-ringleted little girl, arms outstretched, no longer sick, running toward her through the clouds.

Mirror, Mirror

Ganny didn't talk very much about her childhood. She was never one for self-analysis and maintained a special loathing for all manner of bragging and complaining. If guests came over and went on and on about themselves, whether about their problems or their achievements, as soon as they left, Ganny would exclaim, "How *boring*!"

She lived by her own law. In those final years, her back pain was so severe that she had a hard time bending over to pick up a dropped book or to pet her beloved lapdogs Mini and Bibi—but she never spoke of this aloud. The only reason I knew about her back trouble at all is because my father told me that she whispered an explanation for her labored movements to him, her eldest son, out of earshot of other family members. He later told me that when she said she was in pain she sounded slightly ashamed, as if her failure to conquer the discomfort were a failure of will. She always wanted to be strong for us. To her, that meant never asking for help or admitting to frailty.

I sometimes sensed that there was genuine pain lurking behind her stoicism, particularly when it came to her past. While she never discussed such matters with me when I was young, later in her life when I had children of my own, she opened up a little bit. I imagine she had reached a point when she felt compelled to share the stories of her youth, and I was an eager audience. I was curious to know what early experiences might have helped make her into our indomitable matriarch.

Early one day in Maine, I asked Ganny about her childhood. Ganny answered frankly. Born in New York City but raised in the suburb of Rye, New York, she was the third of four children. She adored her father, Marvin Pierce, nicknamed Monk, and longed to be just like him.

"He was so tall and handsome," she told me wistfully, her face suddenly losing years, her hazel eyes filling with light.

As a young man, Marvin was considered one of the finest athletes to attend Miami of Ohio. As an adult, he was president of the McCall Corporation, which published *Redbook* and *McCall's* magazines. And he was an attentive father. He took time to talk to his daughter openly and honestly about her life. She loved how he treated her like an equal.

Ganny's mother, Pauline, was a renowned beauty. Ganny told me her mother openly favored her gorgeous older sister, Martha, always commenting on her long, lustrous hair and elegant figure. According to Ganny, as a young woman she was plump in comparison to her sister and far preferred sports to fashion. At the dinner table, Pauline often told Martha to eat more and my grandma to eat less.

Listening to my strong Ganny say these words made my heart hurt. Imagining young Barbara Pierce, with her quick wit and brilliant brain, reduced to her body shape, compared unfavorably with her thinner sister, was almost too much to bear.

Ganny's other siblings, too, received more attention than she did. Her brother Scott, five years younger, spent his early childhood in and out of hospitals because of a dangerous bone cyst. Jimmy, three years older, was a lovable rascal.

When Ganny was twenty-four, living far from home in remote West Texas and pregnant with her second child, Robin, she received a horrible shock. Her parents had been driving in their car in New York when Pauline set down a cup of coffee on the seat. Marvin reached over to steady it and lost control of the car, which hit a tree and stone wall. He survived, but she died in the crash.

Ganny was unable to attend her mother's funeral because she was six months pregnant and had been advised not to travel. Missing the service would always haunt her, as their fraught relationship came to an end without closure.

Marvin's new wife, Willa, whom he married three years later, was no kinder to Ganny about her looks. (She won few friends in the family, too, when she later contributed to Jack Kemp's campaign against her own son-in-law, something that was publicized by the Kemp campaign.)

Even in her nineties, many years after both her sister and her mother had died, Ganny still felt inferior; comments about her appearance still stung. Until she met my grandfather, only her father had ever made her feel seen and loved. It seemed that she was still scarred by her mother's having thought her unattractive—a judgment reinforced every time the press made fun of her fashion choices.

As the sun moved higher in the sky and I sat across from her on the faded blue sofa, she told me that it was simply a matter of fact, not opinion—she was never the pretty one, and "Martha was the true beauty."

I stared at her, agape. This woman had accomplished so much. Her face showed the decades of winter snowstorms and summer suns, the pain of losing a child and the stress of politics, but also the strength of a woman who made the world better and who had experienced lifelong love. She had been the First Lady of the United States! She was one of only two women in history to have her husband and her son become president. She had traveled the world, lived in China. She had adoring children, grandchildren, and great-grandchildren. Untold books and articles had been written about her. And yet the ache resulting from hearing her mother say that her sister was more beautiful seemed never to have left her.

Ganny's mother's words were a personal tragedy for

my grandmother. They also created reverberations felt by others in our family. As so many do, Ganny turned her feelings about her own appearance outward, critiquing those she loved best. If she thought someone was dressed inappropriately or if their body did not look its best, she let them know. If Barbara or I wore cutoff jean shorts, Ganny scolded us. If one of her sons seemed to be developing a paunch, he would hear about it from her. Would a great-granddaughter get away with wearing a crop top in her presence? Absolutely not!

When I was nineteen and sitting by her pool in Maine, clad in a yellow bikini (and greased up, I'm sure, with some ungodly tanning oil), Ganny told me how proud she was of the grades I'd received in my first year at UT Austin. Then she said, "You've put on some weight, haven't you?"

I had. I'd gained the usual freshman fifteen, or freshman eighteen, but who was counting? Still, her pointing it out hurt my feelings. I tugged at my bikini, silently wishing it would hide more of me, wanting the cover-up I had left in my room. Now, though, I know that when she spoke about my weight it was her mother's voice speaking through her, admonishing her own teenage self.

There was irony there, of course. Even as she scolded us for not keeping better control over our bodies, Ganny let herself age. She embraced her wrinkles. She'd let her hair go white in her forties. *Botox* was not a word—let alone a product—she'd ever use. Especially as someone in the public eye, she was brave to let nature take its course. She famously said that people who worried about their hair were boring. When pundits said she looked older than her husband during the 1988 campaign, she told a reporter, "I'm not going to turn into a glamorous princess. I'm not going to worry about it. I have plenty of self-confidence, not in how I look but in how I feel." She said she felt good about her husband, her children, and her life.

And she did feel good about those things. Still, I could see that she carried a lifelong insecurity about her looks, too, and I blame her mother for that. I feel fortunate that my parents never put pressure on Barbara and me to look any particular way. They may have raised their eyebrows at an odd outfit here or there, but they always told us we were beautiful, no matter our weight. Our mother never dieted. She didn't keep junk food in the house, but that was only because she didn't want to eat it. She definitely wasn't the type to ever say, "I look fat," or "This doesn't look good on me." Looking back, I think it was a conscious effort on her part to model a healthy body image for my sister and me.

Yet from a young age, I felt chubby. In my fourth grade diary, my New Year's resolution was to lose weight. Now I want to hug that little girl. I can't bear to think about my beautiful daughters ever feeling that way. I want them to love the way they look and to take gaining and losing weight as an inevitable part of being a human living in the world, rather than as a moral failing. I am careful never to use words like *fat* or *skinny,* or to make them overly conscious of their bodies or their appetites.

I did tell Mila over Christmas, "You've had ice cream every day of vacation, but remember, we're not going to have dessert every day when we get home to New York."

So far I would say she does not seem to be neurotic about food, because her reaction to this was the indignant reply: "How dare you put me on a *diet*!"

At a family dinner in Houston after Ganny's funeral, my aunt Doro and I talked about Ganny in all her might and all her acerbity. And Doro told me a story. She talked about arriving in Houston with nothing black to wear for the funeral. Shopping at the local mall, she found a dress she loved, but she worried that it was too expensive. She thought, *Gosh, Mom would hate this dress. She would think it was too showy.* Ganny was frugal; she would think it had cost far too much. Doro went ahead and splurged on the dress. Once at her parents' house, she put it on again and went to admire herself in the mirror. It was a beautiful dress. She felt good that she'd bought—

At that moment, the mirror fell off the wall.

Doro thought her mother was sending her a clear sign: *Yes, I hate it! Too expensive!* And Doro returned the dress.

I set down my fork and put my hand on Doro's. As the buzz of our relatives' conversation and the clinking of silverware continued around us, I told her that I interpreted the falling mirror in another way. I saw it as a sign that Ganny did not want Doro to worry about her clothes or her looks for one more second. I told Doro I thought Ganny was saying, *Don't look at the mirror anymore. If I ever said anything that hurt you, that's because of my mother. You are beautiful. Wear whatever makes you feel good. Spend money now if you like, because you can't take it with you. Enjoy your one wild and precious life.*

Doro did not seem completely convinced, but she said that could be one way to interpret the falling mirror.

As I lay in bed that night, I said a prayer to my grandmother. I told her, "Thank you for seeing that all the women you love deserve to be free of the shame and distraction that might otherwise keep us from enjoying the blessings of this life."

I told her, too, that I hoped she was now able to hear a voice louder than her mother's and her stepmother's. I hoped that those fusty old calls to diet, to wear more makeup, or to try to look younger, slimmer, more alluring, were being drowned out by the strong, sure voices of her besotted husband, of her devoted children and grandchildren and friends, and of those thousands of mourners at St. Martin's. I hoped she could finally hear our voices raised in her honor. I hoped she could at last believe what we told her—that to us she was among the most beautiful women who ever lived.

The Greatest Gift

Dear Ganny,

Today is my birthday. You know that, of course. You were always so good about marking every holiday, every special occasion. Now that you're gone, I feel your absence most strongly on these days. Where once there was a letter from you, now there is a void. I felt this void first this summer in Maine. We all did. Walking onto the porch one day, I accidentally slammed the screen door (which still needs to be oiled, by the way). I cringed at the loud *thwap*. Then I waited to hear your voice calling out from the other room: "Jen, try not to slam the door. Gamps is asleep." But instead of your voice, I heard only silence.

On that trip, whenever we left wet shoes or sandy towels on the floor after returning from the beach, I started to walk away from the mess but then thought of your rules and returned to clear them away. I looked around, eager to have you catch me doing the right thing. But you were nowhere to be seen.

As we sat around the dinner table talking at night, there was no mediator and no pot-stirrer (you could be either or both, depending on the day!). Conversations—polite, measured, respectful—felt flat.

Your absence in death looms as large for me as your presence did in life. On my thirty-seventh birthday, I keep thinking of all you'd done by the time you were this age. It was 1962. You'd seen the love of your life go off to war and come home safely. You'd been married for seventeen years. You'd given birth to six children and buried one of them. You'd lost your mother. Your hair had turned silver.

There is still so much I have to learn from your resilience, from your courage, from your wisdom. I wish you were here.

Love,

Jenna

Of course, I share my birthday with another Barbara. My sister proudly bears our grandmother's moniker, a once-popular name some say is slowly going extinct. Our birthday always falls right around Thanksgiving. Our mother, who spent the end of her pregnancy on bed rest for preeclampsia, recalls eating turkey and mashed potatoes in the hospital. She told us that Thanksgiving was the perfect season for having babies, because of the gratitude she felt when she held a baby in each arm. At such moments, she sighed and thought, *This is the life.*

On my thirty-seventh birthday, I had my own two babies, beautiful girls whom I love more than life. And yet my gratefulness was waning. I'd spent the holidays in a small town in West Virginia with Henry, the girls, and my in-laws. We stayed at a hotel that was the children's dream; there was an indoor pool smelling of chlorine. That meant I'd wrestled little limbs into and out of their one-pieces several times a day. And now, on the day of my birth, we were in transit. I was running through Dulles Airport trying to make a connection to JFK with two squirming, grubby toddlers. We were tired, homesick, and covered head to toe in Goldfish cracker dust. Happy birthday to me.

On the flight, we were seated in the second-to-last row, right next to the toilets, in a vortex of toddler squabbles, broken iPad headphones, and crumbs welded to every surface by spilled ginger ale. A flight attendant who'd overheard us talking leaned over and handed me champagne in a plastic cup. I locked eyes with her and mouthed, "Thank you." She whispered back, "Happy birthday."

Arriving home that evening, Henry and I collapsed in an exhausted heap. With great effort, we got the girls settled, and then we started going through the pile of mail on our front table. Even the act of opening envelopes felt like work. It was the usual medley of bills, invites, and junk. But among the detritus was a box from my aunt Doro.

I opened it, pushed away the tissue paper, and said, "Oh, Henry, look! These are from my grandmother!"

Doro had sent three things. I held up the first one, a clown ornament needlepointed by my Ganny.

"That clown looks demonic," Henry said.

"Henry! Ganny loved needle-pointing ornaments! We have to put it on our Christmas tree."

(He was right, though. With its piercing eyes and too-red smiling mouth, it looked uncannily like Pennywise from *It*.)

Henry merely raised his eyebrows, wisely choosing not to fight me on it.

The next item out of the box was a well-worn purple clutch purse that I'd seen Ganny use many times in the past. I think she particularly liked the fake-pearl clasp. I turned it over and thought of seeing her hands pulling out a mint to offer to a grandchild or great-grandchild in church or at a play in the hope that it would keep them quiet. One was never far away!

The final memento to emerge was a pashmina I'd seen Ganny wear. I smelled it and my eyes filled with tears.

"What does it smell like?" Henry asked. "Why are you sniffing it?"

"It smells like her," I said.

I received this thoughtful care package when I needed comfort the most. The items themselves were not important, and yet they each seemed to whisper to me, "Here's a little something to cheer you up on this special day."

Ganny was a prolific letter writer. She wrote me on every special occasion but also on plenty of ordinary days: when she wanted to say hello or let me know she had seen me on TV; to thank me for this or say I was welcome for that; or to catch me up on some gossip. This was the first year in thirty-seven that I had not received a letter or a card from her. And yet, thanks to my aunt, here were things she had touched, things that had been hers. It felt to me like they came straight from her.

When I closed my eyes and inhaled her scent, it seemed as though she was there with me. It was a sign from Ganny.

I believe in signs. Yes, my aunt Doro had sent the package, simply out of the goodness of her heart. And yet the timing and the power of that gift was more than even she was capable of alone. I believe people we love go to heaven and there are still signs of them everywhere we look.

I received a sign earlier this year at my therapist's office. I see a therapist who's also a healer. In addition to helping me talk through my problems, she leads me in breathing exercises and meditation. I always leave feeling lighter and more centered.

In this particular session, I was newly pregnant, not yet showing. I spoke about my anxieties for the baby's health and how I worried that my fear might keep me from connecting to him the way I had to Mila and Poppy, with whom I felt fully bonded the second I learned I was pregnant.

"We're going to make sure you connect with the baby,"

my therapist said. "Don't worry." And at the end of our conversation, she gave me an active breathing exercise to do before leaving. In the middle of the breathing exercise I felt hands on my stomach. *How sweet,* I thought. *Christine is touching my belly so I'll feel less anxious! What a lovely woman. And what strong, comforting hands she has!* Another minute passed this way, and then I heard something fall near Christine's desk.

"Sorry!" Christine said from the desk side of the room.

My eyes shot open. The feeling of the hands instantly disappeared.

"I just felt hands on my belly," I said. "That wasn't you?"

Christine said no, but she was delighted to hear I'd had that feeling. She is a trained minister who believes that there is life after death and that those we love are still part of our world. She asked me if I felt the presence of anyone in particular.

I thought about it. Whose strong hands were those? My mind kept drifting to Pa, who loved children and who I knew would want to keep me and my child safe. I don't know exactly what comes after death, but I do know that on that day I needed to feel reassurance about my pregnancy, and someone or something gave me that comfort. I left feeling that all my grandparents were looking down from somewhere, reassuring me and my baby.

What a wonderful feeling to know that through the lessons they taught me and by their enduring presence in my heart and maybe in spirit, they continue to be there for me and for us all.

"I Know You Miss Them, Too"

From the earliest I can remember, I knew my grandparents were in love. They wrote each other letters filled with romance and longing when they were young—and later in life, love emails. They held hands under the dining room table. If I ever expected one of them to side with me against the other, I was always disappointed.

After Ganny died, we thought Gampy would miss her so much he wouldn't live long without her. And in fact, two days after her funeral, he was hospitalized. His heart stopped twice, only to be revived.

"His heart is broken," I told Barbara.

He made it clear, though, that he wanted to spend one more summer in Maine, his other great love.

His last summer in Maine, he watched his great-grandchildren play and the surf crash every morning onto the rocks. And in the fall, he watched my sister, his granddaughter, marry her true love. He soaked in every moment of life in that place that for us symbolizes the eternal constant of family.

At my sister's wedding, I often hid my face from my grandfather so that he would not see me wiping away tears. Once the most powerful man in the world, now he was in a wheelchair. Once the leader of our family, the undisputed patriarch, the man we went to when we had dreams to share or advice to seek now seemed weary, as though the value in each day came from its bringing him that much closer to being reunited with the woman he loved for every minute of their seventy-three-year marriage.

What eased these moments of heartache were my girls. They did not predict, like the rest of us, that he would not live to see another summer in Maine. They saw only that their beloved Great-Gampy was tired. Their mission was to make him laugh. They said, often, "We need to go and hug Great-Gampy!" or "Is Great-Gampy awake? Let's go tell him good morning!"

The last summer with him I was struck by the contrast between my girls' bright, innocent laughter and the weight of knowing that my Gampy's life was coming to an end.

Every summer, I've gone with my grandparents to their lifelong Maine church, St. Ann's Episcopal. This sea-washed stone chapel, built in 1892, is where on rainy days as a little girl I stared out the stained-glass window, wishing the sermon was over so I could go and splash in the puddles. On cloudless days, during the outside services, I looked at the ocean, counting boats and lobster pots as the minister preached. As a young adult, I saw my cousins marry at this very altar. As a mother, I had my babies baptized outside by the sea, my grandparents looking on. Now I try to quiet my children as they squirm or try to run to the seawall, just as my grandparents shushed me thirty-five years ago.

Last summer, for the first time in memory, my grandfather was too sick to go with us to church. After church each Sunday, my father asked Peter Cheney, St. Ann's chaplain, to come to our house after services. Before lunch, we went to my grandfather's room, where Reverend Cheney led us in the Communion service. My grandfather, dressed for the day and sitting up in his brown corduroy recliner, eagerly accepted the wafer from the priest's hand.

One Sunday that summer Reverend Cheney did something different. After we read the Eucharist service and Gampy took the wafer, Reverend Cheney suggested we all sing a hymn together. We asked Gampy what he wanted to sing. I thought he might choose an Episcopal church standard—perhaps "Amazing Grace" or "Lift High the Cross" or "Come Thou Long Expected Jesus." He surprised us all by choosing "Jesus Loves Me," the first religious song many of us who grow up Christian ever learn.

We all knew the song, of course, but many of us hadn't sung it since childhood. Our voices faltering, we joined Gampy's and sang it the best we could remember, with

the ocean waves crashing outside the window as accom-
paniment.

> *Jesus loves me—this I know,*
> *For the Bible tells me so;*
> *Little ones to Him belong—*
> *They are weak but He is strong.*

Before we were halfway through the song, we were
fighting back tears, not making eye contact for fear our
emotion would be contagious. The song we'd once sung
unthinkingly now carried a message of love and triumph
that we needed to hear.

> *Jesus loves me—loves me still,*
> *Though I'm very weak and ill.*

This once-strong man we loved was now weak. And
yet he showed us by his song choice that he did not feel
ashamed of his infirmity. He felt that God loved him in his
frailty as much as he had loved him as a leader of millions.

> *Jesus loves me—He will stay,*
> *Close beside me all the way;*
> *He's prepared a home for me,*
> *And some day His face I'll see.*

At the end of the song, all of us were emotional. I
clutched a needlepoint pillow that my grandmother had

made—its sentiment, "Reading is sexy," made me smile— and faced my Ganny's garden, where she could no longer be seen pruning her roses. We knew Gampy would join her soon. Singing with him that day, we felt like children again, and we felt God's love fill the room.

One of the last times I saw my grandfather alive was in this same bedroom. This is where at the end of a long day he and my Ganny sat quietly together, he reading histories and she meticulously needlepointing Christmas stockings for her great-grandchildren. When they grew older, they listened to beloved audiobooks and watched TV crime shows.

Summer after summer, this was where they slept side by side, their hands entwined.

I saw myself as a little girl and as a teenager and— most unbelievably—as a mother. Now my rambunctious girls pulled me into this same room, saying, "We have to say goodbye to Great-Gampy before we leave, Mama!"

Saying goodbye. To my children, this was just one more goodbye. They believed there would be many more hellos to come. It was hard for me to be around my grandpa because I knew that he would soon be leaving us, but Mila and Poppy had no such distraction. All children know is that this person they love is here and they want to hug him, to tell him about their day at the beach, to say they love him and will see him again soon.

In his room, Mila and Poppy clambered up on Gampy's lap, in the chair where he sat most days. By his feet, swollen from age and wear, sat his precious service dog, Sully.

My little girls—Poppy, with charisma like his; Mila, with his gentleness and empathy—wrapped their arms around him. Their milky arms served as a stark contrast to his arms, wrinkled and full of age spots, signs of a life spent outdoors. Their youth, his age. Their innocence, his wisdom. Their movements jumpy and urgent, his slow. He was tired, but his eyes brightened with life when they entered the room. He smiled as they petted his hands. He seemed almost like a child. His purity came from God as much as theirs.

"They are beautiful," he whispered.

To see them together was more than I could bear. I stepped outside to let my tears fall in private. Standing there in the yard, I remembered one of my grandfather's rules: "You will cry when you are happy and also when you are sad." I was both. I felt too much.

In that moment, I felt joy to think of what the future held for my beautiful, tender girls and heartbroken that my Gampy would not be with us much longer. He would not see them grow into young women. He would not be there to give them advice when they had their first break-ups, nor would he attend their weddings.

I thought of something my Gampy told me when we were visiting him in the ICU at the hospital. I was pregnant with Mila, glowing with that feeling that often comes from a first pregnancy. How hard it was to see suffering when I was flush with the promise of new life. With Mila growing inside me, I felt I was in possession of the best secret in the world. And then Gampy touched my stomach, whispering, "There is death and then there is life."

Death and life. How poignant it was on that summer day to see them sitting side by side. Old age and youth on the same chair. An end and a beginning.

Just months later, Henry and I attended Gampy's funeral. We decided the girls were too young to attend in person, so we left them for the day with Henry's mother. She showed them the funeral on television and told us later that they were a bit confused by it. When my father turned around in the chapel to wave to a friend, Mila thought it was she he was waving at, through the TV. Poppy kept saying, "Why is Gampy in the box?"

I winced when I heard this. I wondered if we should not have let them watch, even on TV.

But how much can you shelter your children when everyone around them is in mourning? They learned about death this year, my little girls. Too young, they became wise. One night after Ganny and Gampy had both passed, I peeked into Mila's room. In her raspy voice, she whispered, "Mama, come sit with me."

I sat on the edge of her bed.

"I miss them," she said. "I miss Great-Ganny and Great-Gampy. And I know you miss them, too."

She was quiet for a moment, and then she asked, "Mama, are you going to die?"

"Not for a long time," I said.

"Mama, am *I* going to die?" she said.

"Not for a *very* long time," I said. I hoped I was doing enough to reassure her.

"I know, Mama, but when I do, I won't be sad because I will see them again and I will see you."

After a few minutes, Mila continued. "Mama, what do you think heaven is like?"

I told her I didn't know. I stared at my little girl's face, aglow from the streetlights. She was so young, yet here she was comforting her mother. I wondered where that grace came from—and in her bright, kind eyes I saw Gampy.

Summer Rain

When we lived in Texas, my family attended church almost every week. I enjoyed going, though not because I was particularly devout. I was a chubby foodie (before *foodie* was a word) and went to church without kicking or screaming because afterward we went out for waffles covered in whipped cream and chocolate sauce at Roscoe White's Easy Way Café. When I was older, the highlight of my confirmation retreat was, well, the boys—and one in particular, Jeff, the camp bad boy, who brought cigarettes, hidden under his Bible.

The place I finally found God, without any hope for some immediate earthly reward in the form of carbs or boys, was at a secular camp my father went to as a little boy and I attended as well, Camp Longhorn.

The summer after my freshman year of high school was a transformational time. My fellow cabinmates and I were cauldrons of teen drama and hormones. We had the Beatles' *Abbey Road* on constant repeat, our moods careening between "Carry That Weight" and "Here Comes the Sun."

When my high school boyfriend sent me flowers with a note testifying to his longing and devotion, someone in my cabin threw his gift on the ground outside. Who knows why? Envy or boredom, probably. Was it an accident? Who knows? It didn't matter. My ensuing despair was off the charts. The dramatic weeping and wailing were such that you'd think I was Job, rather than a fifteen-year-old girl prevented from fully enjoying a bouquet of cheap carnations.

As little girls at Camp Longhorn, we'd played pickleball and had swim races. Now, as teens, we played new games—games such as who could overreact the most to a borrowed hairbrush or who could be more traumatized by a perceived insult.

One girl in our cabin, whom I'll call Kelly, took no part in these hysterics. And yet she seemed sadder than any of us, lost in her headphones and her private pain—related, we were told, to some difficulties her family was having. It was clear to anyone who looked in her eyes that she was hurting badly.

Kelly had trouble sleeping, and sometimes she refused to get out of bed in the morning to go to the required activities. While we went out to swim or sail or laugh over our bowls of cereal, she stayed in bed. We'd also started to notice that she was developing scabs on her arms and legs, scabs unlike the ones the rest of us had from our encounters with brambles and gravel. Eventually we realized that these wounds were self-inflicted. She was cutting herself.

We didn't understand her despair. The teenager we saw was not the girl we had known all those years. Just the summer before, Kelly had been a rambunctious eighth grader, her eyes filled with light. Now she told us she was tired and wanted to be alone. We felt powerless.

One day, when we returned to our cabin, we found Kelly sitting on her metal bunk bed. She had carved the word *HELP* into her arm and was bleeding heavily. We ran for help. The camp administrators called her parents and told them there was an emergency. They came to pick her up. She went home for the rest of the summer.

We, her cabinmates and friends, were devastated and confused. We had never experienced pain like that; this was beyond our comprehension. We wondered both how we'd failed her and how someone could hurt so much. As we packed up Kelly's things for her, a Texas summer storm raged outside. We tried to make sense of her pain. After her departure, we sat in a circle—asking questions, leaning on one another—for the rest of the afternoon. The sound of thunder provided a soundtrack to our melancholy. Flashes of lightning illuminated the tear-soaked faces of girls I had known since first grade.

Finally, depleted, we left our cabin to walk to the cafeteria for dinner. The storm had stopped. In the sky, a rainbow stretched over the lake. Until that day, the rainbows I'd seen had been faint or fleeting. This one was strong and clear—each color a bold bright stripe. The rainbow glistened and glowed so deeply that I gasped upon seeing it and could not turn my eyes away.

The wet grass smelled fresh and new. I breathed in deeply. To me, it was the scent of hope and promise, and of comfort in the face of pain. It reminded me of "Hymn of Promise," which we sang at the funeral for my grandfather Harold, the first person I loved and lost:

> *In the bulb there is a flower;*
> *in the seed, an apple tree;*
> *in cocoons, a hidden promise:*
> *butterflies will soon be free!*

Gazing at the rainbow, I felt my heart fill with hope. After the deepest pain, here was an offering of peace. There was no question in my mind that God had put this rainbow in the sky.

Back in the cabin that night, I wrote a letter to my father by flashlight. I said I'd been grappling with the question of how someone who was loved could still want to hurt herself. I told him about the rainbow that made me feel the presence of God.

"Dear Dad," I wrote. "There must be a God. This comfort was a sign."

From that day on, I knew that there had to be a greater purpose to suffering. Faith to me is not loud or boisterous; it is simply the belief that no pain exists that God cannot take away. I feel the same surety that no matter how difficult something is, God will provide the answer.

When my father picked me up from the last day of camp weeks later—with my boyfriend from home in tow!—he told me how happy he had been to receive that letter.

My father has always been open about his faith. For him, it was talking to Billy Graham and quitting drinking that brought him closer to God. He had his epiphany when he was forty and worried that his life wasn't going the way he'd hoped. He started reading the Bible every morning before beginning work to center himself, and he's kept up that habit to this day.

I never saw Kelly again. I've often wondered what happened to her. Now, twenty years later, my congregation reads together from *The Book of Common Prayer:* "Comfort and heal all those who suffer in body, mind, or spirit; give them courage and hope in their troubles, and bring them the joy of your salvation."

Amen.

"Poor Henry"

Some women struggle because their parents don't fully accept their husbands. I have the opposite problem. My parents adore Henry. They praise him and sympathize with him. In fact, "Poor Henry" is one of their refrains. Another is "Saint Henry."

When Henry and I were still dating, my mom was asked by a reporter when Henry and I were going to get engaged. Flustered and trying to preserve our privacy, she answered, "They aren't that serious." Henry read that in the paper and it hurt his feelings. We had been discussing marriage.

My mom has more than made up for her accidentally hurtful comment as the years have gone by. When he proposed, she was thrilled, and her adoration has only grown as she's seen him in action as a husband and father.

At a recent talk I gave with my mom and sister at a women's panel in Dallas, my mom told the audience, "Our son-in-law Henry is a saint. He's home with the kids while Jenna is here."

There is an unwelcome undertone to her portrayal of Henry as a saint. The corollary is that being married to me is akin to the martyrdom experienced by the saints. I have been to church. I know what some of those saints endured. Comparing marriage to me with the torments undergone by the holy stings a bit.

What's more, the context of the Dallas speech was rather ironic. There we were, ostensibly discussing the power of women. My mother was describing my husband as a martyr for doing basic child care.

"Mom!" I said. "This is not the fifties! Henry is not a saint just because I travel for work. Besides, he is not at home with the kids, mopping the floors and ironing our sheets. He is at work. The kids are at school."

The audience laughed. Mom smiled and shrugged. There is no arguing with her when it comes to Henry's perfection. She always said that she'd prefer her children marry an Eagle Scout than marry a prince. Henry is an honest-to-goodness Eagle Scout.

She also finds Henry's long history of ailments and injuries to be hilarious. In our family, you never discuss your pain, but Henry feels very free to discuss his health issues. Since I've known him, his complaints have included: hay fever, being whacked by the door of a Secret Service car while biking, a pulled shoulder, a pulled hamstring, a pulled back muscle, a pulled neck muscle, a torn elbow, a torn shoulder, a torn hamstring, a sprained ankle, a sprained wrist, an allergy to cats, and insomnia.

One evening during the holidays, Barbara, Henry, and I came home early. We heard music coming from the Treaty Room. My mom and her friends were still up listening to music and dancing. Embarrassed (and inspired) that our sixty-year-old mother was outpartying us, we joined in the merriment.

Barbara and I have a signature dance move: the Bucking Bronco. We pretend one of us is the horse and the other is the rider. On this occasion, we turned Henry into our horse. We yelled, "Bucking Bronco! Bucking Bronco!" Henry, eager to please, bucked. Barbara flew off his back and landed on his leg, which resulted in a stress fracture. At the Christmas party the next day, he wore a boot and walked with a cane. Poor, poor Henry.

THERE WAS A moment during our first year of marriage when I did feel sorry for Henry.

That first year was, shall we say, challenging. I cursed the stories I'd heard about how the first year of marriage is one long honeymoon. I remember standing in the kitchen of our tiny Baltimore townhouse. We bickered about one thing or the other, and I always thought, *Screw Jane Austen! This is not the stuff of* Pride and Prejudice*!*

To some extent, Henry had known what he was in for. When Henry and I married, he was marrying the president's daughter. My dowry consisted of unlimited White House visits, but the tax on this privilege was steep. As public figures, we were tabloid fodder, and strangers often speculated about our lives.

There were, of course, also security concerns, not that we paid much attention. What we did not fully realize was how much of a buffer the Secret Service afforded us. The agents were omnipresent at the beginning of our relationship. They were with us on our first date, at our engagement, at our wedding, on our honeymoon, and at our first home in Baltimore.

Then they were gone. The children of presidents retain protection for only six months after the next president is inaugurated. In the first year of our marriage, the Secret Service and their black Suburbans disappeared. Henry, the Eagle Scout, the protector, realized that it was now up to him to keep us—read: *me*—safe.

This may not seem like a significant challenge, but then the Maryland newspaper *The Daily Record* printed the address of the Federal Hill townhouse where we lived.

Federal Hill is a vibrant historic neighborhood in downtown Baltimore. There are gorgeous views of the harbor, as well as a great farmers' market that's been open since 1846. There are also bars—a lot of bars—from craft brewhouses to cocktail rooms to pizza pubs. And after *The Daily Record* revealed our address, we became a stop on many revelers' bar crawls.

One time, after a long day of work, Henry and I were asleep, and then—*boom, boom, boom!*—a loud, menacing series of knocks on the door roused us.

Henry leaped from the bed and raced toward the sound,

charging the front door, only to discover that the drunks had fled.

During our dating years and the early days of our marriage, there had been a buffer of men with guns in fanny packs. Now all of a sudden our lives were in the hands of Henry Chase Hager. He had mastered outdoor skills, but he wasn't trained in hand-to-hand combat. When he'd told my parents at our wedding, "I will always protect your daughter," he'd meant it. With the Secret Service gone, though, that burden was much greater.

For months we jumped at every knock on the door. Eventually the nightly visitations petered out. We resumed the normal business of being a married couple.

Many things are easier more than a decade into marriage. Many things are not. One topic of dissent between us: Henry hates social media. I don't. I tell myself that I need it for work, but the truth is that I love seeing photos of my friends' children.

About a year ago—in the interest of our safety and, well, respecting our kids' privacy—Henry went on an all-out campaign to get the family off the internet. This struck me as extreme. He's already nearly invisible online.

As a rule, I avoid posting photos of him, but one day I couldn't help myself. Henry had been on a trip, and upon his return he'd brought calla lilies for the girls. Poppy was delighted. I took a photo of Henry and Poppy posing with the bouquet and put it up on Instagram with the caption "Look who's home after a week of work! #daddyboy #twins."

I used #twins because the two of them have nearly identical features. And I used #daddyboy because it's the nickname the girls use for him.

Unfortunately, as I quickly learned, #daddyboy has another meaning: it's a term for role play involving one older and one younger man. Some followers of mine seemed concerned. When I clicked on the hashtag, the most recent #daddyboy photos were of muscle-bound men wearing thongs on the beach—and then there was the photo of my husband with our child. I deleted the hashtag, but the photo was already tagged with it, so I wound up deleting the whole post.

As Henry isn't on Instagram (or any social media for that matter), I thought he would never know about this incident, but apparently the image got picked up by a news site and Henry saw it. I told him he should feel pleased by the warm feedback on the picture and at his rapid acceptance into the #daddyboy community.

Poor Henry.

He asked for more photo approval on social media going forward.

Poor me.

My Girls as Sisters

Nothing makes me happier than seeing my girls whispering together. I think, as I watch their precious faces close together, *You don't yet know how lucky you are that you have each other. You will see each other through love and through pain. And you will be by each other's side, whatever comes.*

They have an innate love for each other the way Barbara and I have always had. Of course there are arguments over things like who gets to play with the coveted red-haired mermaid Barbie or who gets to sit on my lap for story time. But their deep love endures.

I love how they are their own people already. Mila is soft-spoken, with a raspy voice I like to think she gets from me. She is a true first child—deeply serious about responsibility, afraid to break rules. Her biggest fear is going to the principal's office, though her teachers insist she is in no danger of that. At a recent parent-teacher conference, a teacher told us, "Mila rebelled a little bit, and we're so proud of her!"

I know, I know: wait until she turns sixteen. If she's anything like me, she will rebel plenty, and neither her teachers nor her parents will find it adorable. For now, though, I marvel every day at her delicate, open nature, which leads her to say things like "Mommy, I'm crying because it's been too long since I had a good cry."

That's her lovely, sensitive Great-Gampy in her, I think.

Of course she is not always perfect. For one thing, she is a stickler when it comes to beauty standards.

The other morning, I cooked the girls eggs while dancing along to Taylor Swift. *I'm such a fun mom!* I thought.

Then as I slid their perfectly cooked eggs onto their BPA-free plates, Mila said, "What are those red things on your face?"

I decided that the science behind hormonal acne in the eighth month of pregnancy was too complex, so I said, "Just a few bumps because I'm pregnant, honey!"

She replied, "I don't like it! I'm not having breakfast until you go put makeup on!"

She came on TV with me one day to help introduce Sully, my grandfather's service dog. Backstage, she sought out the most beautiful girl who works on the show, Donna, whose complexion—glowing olive skin, paired with silky dark hair—is the opposite of mine.

"Donna," she said, "when Mommy dies, will you be my stepmother?"

Later, when I recounted the story to Barbara, Barbara

said that Mila had made her the same stepmother offer. Thanks a lot, Disney.

When I asked her about it, Mila was reassuring. She said, "Don't worry, Mom! I won't love my stepmother as much as I love you."

I wanted to reply, "Oh, honey, if your dad is like a lot of men, your stepmother hasn't even been born yet." With uncharacteristic restraint, I held that thought inside so as not to scar her.

Poppy, Mila's little sister, is not yet old enough to beauty-shame me, but she is still a force to be reckoned with. Her personality is bouncy and bright. She makes herself known. She was named after my grandfather, whose pre-Gampy nickname was Poppy, and the name suits her. She ricochets around a room like popcorn popping in a pot with no lid.

When Poppy was a newborn, Mila looked at the sea of babies in the nursery and picked Poppy out right away. It may have helped that Mila's photograph was taped with care on Poppy's bassinet, but we chose to believe that it was their profound instant connection. Then, soon after we brought her home, Mila started chanting, "Poopy Poppy!"

It was a brilliant observation. Diaper-related occasions were a huge percentage of Poppy's day, after all. But it made Henry and me panic about her name. Were kids going to call Poppy that for the rest of her life?

We worried, too, when friends thought her name was

"Puppy," thanks to how the name sounded to them in my slight Texas accent. "What a . . . *spirited* name," one ventured, before I corrected her and she said, "Oh, thank goodness."

As they've gotten older, I'm happy to say that Mila's enthusiasm for her sister's potential has continued. I will overhear Mila say, while looking at her sister's drawing, "Poppy, that capital *P* is beautiful!"

When I go to look, I see a *P* that is entirely age-appropriate for a two-year-old: crooked and facing the wrong way.

Emboldened by the flood of praise from her big sister, Poppy, now four years old, is far from shy. On a recent visit to Mila's elementary school, Poppy said that she'd like to go there when it was time for prekindergarten. As her sister's class was lining up in the hallway, Poppy saluted the older kids from inside the elevator and yelled, as the doors were closing, "See y'all when I'm older!"

On a family drive when Poppy was a baby, Mila looked at her sister, so tiny in her infant car seat, unable even to lift her head, and said, "Mommy, I think Poppy is going to rule the world!"

Looking into the rearview mirror, choked up with emotion, I said to Mila, "Yes, Mila! Maybe Poppy will rule the world." After letting that sink in for a moment, I said, "Maybe one day Poppy could be the president of the United States!"

Mila laughed, and then it was her turn to pause. Finally she said, as if I were stupid and required instruction, "No, Mommy! Presidents are men!"

I glared at Henry—the nearest man—sitting in the driver's seat.

"Don't look at me that way!" Henry said with a defensive laugh. "I didn't tell her that!"

Then I whispered to him so the girls wouldn't hear: "It's depressing that she thinks that, but, Henry, can you believe it? We should really get her into gifted and talented right away. She's not yet three and she knows the presidents!"

"Slow down, Jenna," Henry said. "She knows *two* presidents—her grandfather and her great-grandfather. They're both men. That's why she said that. She's bright, but she's not a *genius*."

Mila might not be ready for college yet. I still love her enthusiasm for her sister and her sister's love for her. When I see the girls cheer for each other, I think that together they really could rule the world.

The Stone Ring

As a child, Henry scoured the beach on Martha's Vineyard with his mother and grandmother, looking for wishing stones—pebble-sized rocks ringed with a line of white quartz. To qualify as a wishing stone, the white quartz line needed to be complete, with no breaks or pauses. He would quietly say his wish to himself before skipping it across the water's edge. Henry's joy at these outings was compromised by just one thing: he wished his father could join them on the hunt.

Henry has known his dad only in a wheelchair. John was diagnosed with polio at the age of thirty-four in 1973, five years before Henry was born, and he has been paralyzed from the waist down ever since. The way he acquired the disease was wildly unlikely, a million-to-one shot, like winning the worst lottery imaginable.

At the time, John was about to start a new job as executive vice president of the American Tobacco Company. The family had just bought a house in Connecticut. They had one baby, Henry's older brother, Jack.

As an infant, Jack was given the oral Sabin polio virus vaccine. He threw up while in his crib in his parents' bedroom. When John cleaned up the vomit, he was unknowingly exposed to the vaccine—and the virus. John had not received sufficient protection himself from the disease, and he became one of the extremely rare cases in which the oral vaccine caused someone to contract it.

Jack was fine, but within days, John began to exhibit the characteristics of someone being attacked by the polio virus. He felt excruciating back pain. His muscles stiffened. He tried to ignore it, but on a run he knocked himself out when he fell unexpectedly. Day after day, he pushed on through the pain, but eventually he was rushed to the emergency room.

For months, John's illness went misdiagnosed. At first doctors thought he had damaged his back while running and they operated to remove several intervertebral discs. That operation left him in more pain, and the stitches soon became infected with gangrene. It wasn't until months later, when Henry's mom, Maggie, got him admitted to the Rusk Institute, that the polio was diagnosed.

John's bosses from the American Tobacco Company sent a representative to visit him in the hospital. They provided financial help, but they also told him that of course it wouldn't be appropriate to have an executive vice president in a wheelchair. They rescinded the job offer. His dream job, his dream home, and his whole life plan were now shattered. The Hagers had to sell the house they had just purchased in Connecticut and move to Virginia.

In 1990, the Americans with Disabilities Act would be signed into law by my grandfather. Under the ADA, John could have filed a lawsuit against his company for employment discrimination. Instead, John resolved to become as physically strong as possible and to work his way back up the chain of command. Back in Virginia, he started as a consultant to the American Tobacco Company. It took him twenty years, but he eventually did become a senior vice president there.

When I learned all this about his father, I understood Henry's burning need to be in constant motion, to achieve, to give back. It's tiring for him—and honestly, for me! But I know it's a result of the pressure of having a dad who, despite living life in a wheelchair, has achieved so much.

Henry grew up as a quietly confident boy. His ears (like my grandfather Harold's) stuck out past his round face. When Henry was eight, his pediatrician offered to pin his ears back. Henry told his mother that he didn't want that, because that's the way God made him.

When Henry was in the fourth grade, he got into a wrestling match with another kid on the playground and bested him. The rival boy was supported by a friend, who decided the best way to get back at him was to throw stones and say, "Well, at least his dad can walk!"

Henry was not a violent child, but he proceeded to punch that boy in the face. The fight was quickly broken up and the boys were ushered to the principal's office. The principal asked for an explanation. After he'd heard both boys' versions of the fight, the principal swiftly excused Henry from his office and kept the other boy for a stern discussion about respect and empathy.

I know Henry thinks a lot about that moment in his life, and so do I. Henry had many beautiful life experiences as a result of growing up with a father in a wheelchair. He may not have been able to hunt for stones on the beach, but John taught his boys patience and understanding and ensured that they knew how to overcome tough odds.

On our ninth anniversary, Henry and I ate outside in a courtyard in a restaurant in Brooklyn. Our May anniversary corresponds with the annual return of outdoor restaurant seating and good weather for long walks through New York City. Henry's gift to me was a wishing-stone ring.

"This is the perfect gift," I told him, "because you are my rock."

It's true. He is stable and solid—the foundation on which our little family relies.

Having a father unable to play football with him or throw him in the air has made Henry appreciate that aspect of fatherhood deeply. I am astonished when I watch Henry chase and tickle the girls. He throws them high in the air as they giggle wildly.

Every day I look at my stone ring and I think, *Thank*

you, Henry. Thank you for throwing our kids in the air in the way your father could not. Thank you for pushing your father up hills. Thank you for making us all laugh. Thank you for this ring, which reminds me every time I look at it that so many of my wishes have already come true.

Dreams of
My Mother

There are traits we pass on to those we love. Yes, genetic gifts: eye color, birthmarks, dimples. But we also share a more ineffable inheritance: our stories, histories, and traditions. Barbara got my mother's piercing blue eyes and I inherited her cheekbones—both characteristics we've come to cherish. She also passed on to Barbara and me her two great loves: cats and books.

When she met my dad, her companionship came with her beloved tuxedo cat Dewey, named after the Dewey decimal system (nerd alert!). Dewey was the head of a long line of cat loves in our family, and he was the one who taught Barbara and me that cats will not hesitate to slap a two-year-old who pulls their tail.

We have had many cats over the years:

Bernadette, also known as Bernie, who is nocturnal and meows wildly at night. When I was pregnant with Mila, I was so miserable because of my inability to take allergy medicine that she had to move in with my mother for the rest of my pregnancy. And then she didn't want to leave.

Sprity, the cat Barbara and I adopted when we were five and named after our favorite soft drink.

Baxter, the furry gray cat who ate dry macaroni and hid sponges under beds.

Mardie, Barbara's beautiful calico cat, named after Mardi Gras. She was hit by a car and then died when the vet tried unsuccessfully to save her by amputating a leg. Her loss broke my sister's heart.

Cowboy, whom I adopted in first grade and named after the Dallas football team.

Ernie, our polydactyl stray, whom we found on the grounds of the governor's mansion and named in honor of Ernest Hemingway and his six-toed cat.

Willard, whose name changed multiple times (other names included Willie and India). She died at the age of fourteen. We fed her steak at the White House as her last meal.

My mom inherited her cat addiction from her mom, Jenna, to whom cats seemed to be drawn—all animals, actually. Henry was my Grammee's cat; he moved over from the neighbors' house because he loved her so much.

My mother, lonely as an only child, loved to read about big families. She wanted to be Jo in *Little Women*. When we were growing up, she didn't talk about her longing for

Kissing my namesake, Jenna Welch—who passed away May 10, 2019.
She taught Barbara and me every constellation in the sky.

a big storm is coming here and
supposidly is going to get bigger than
we haos seen this year!
We miss you and are so proud
of you.
Love to Henry—
Ganny

A note from my
grandmother
Barbara Bush;
all my grandparents
were prolific writers.

Gampy with us on Air Force One. He always
made us feel like we were the most important thing in his life.

Barbara whispers to Barbara during Gampy's inauguration,
January 20, 1989.

We grew up in flat, dusty Midland, Texas; you can tell even from this photo how hot and dry it is during the summers.

Eighties aerobics—exercising on the porch in Maine with a bowl cut.

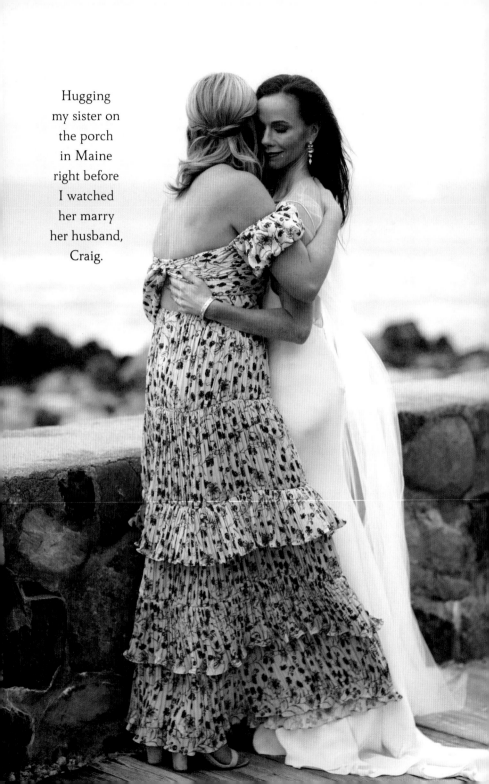

Hugging my sister on the porch in Maine right before I watched her marry her husband, Craig.

Let it snow! My city girls watching the snow fall on our apartment roof in New York City.

Poppy and Poppy! Poppy with my grandfather—for whom she is named.

On our last walk after dinner with
our darling Gamps—his last summer in Maine.

Posing with our grandfather on Barbara's wedding day.

My grandmothers were opposites but they both taught me how to use my voice. Here they are chatting at Henry's and my rehearsal dinner in 2008.

My handsome grandpa Harold Welch
and his beautiful bride, Jenna. This is right
before Harold deployed during WWII.

Reading is in my DNA!
My grandma Jenna reading to my young mom!

Sexting before sexting was a thing! My grandma Jenna took
this bathtub picture to give to her husband while he was away at war.

Walking down the aisle with my sister, Barbara,
and dad to greet Henry on our wedding day.

Thanksgiving Day, surrounded by some of the greatest blessings of my life.

Laughing with Hoda. Her laugh is contagious!

Poppy and Vale share a birthday: August 13.
They also have mothers who are great pals!

Christmas selfie, 2019—poor Henry has
the longest arms and therefore always holds the selfie stick.

#DaddyBoy—my husband,
who is anti–social media,
didn't love that I posted this.

Gone fishing! Henry passing
on one of his greatest loves to Mila.

Poppy on the move—escaping a family Christmas photo!

Oh, boy!! Our family was complete when we had
our baby Henry Harold Hager on August 2, 2019.

a big family, about the fact that her prayer when her mom and dad tucked her in at night was for siblings; that when she blew out birthday candles or wished upon stars, she pictured babies' faces.

Our mom told us often how thrilled she was when the doctor told her she would be having twins. "One for each of us to hold," she said to our father. Until we were adults, she did not tell us how sad she was as a little girl without siblings. But we know now that she found solace in her friendships, cats, and books.

My mom's current love affair is with a cat named Bob. But don't let the simplicity of his name deceive you; their love is complicated and raw. She loves him fully, wholly. Bob showed up at our ranch, a barn cat who, when my mom cradled him in her arms, purred aggressively. For all you fellow cat aficionados out there, my mom says a sign of a loving cat is that he likes to be held like a baby.

My sister and I like to anthropomorphize our family's cats. We ask each other, "What would they be like if they were humans?" and let our imaginations run wild. As kids, we dressed our cats in our T-shirts (yes, they *loved* it). As adults, we affectionately craft elaborate identities for them, including sordid affairs, dramatic accents, and intricate ulterior motives. For example, my cat Bernadette was an eighty-year-old woman from New Jersey who chain-smoked Marlboros.

My mom hates for us to talk about Bob, whom we see as a fabulous fashion designer, always wishing for humans to add more glitter and feathers to their drab wardrobes.

"You don't know Bob the way I do," our mother will say, her eyes narrowing.

"I know Bob thinks you shouldn't wear those shoes with that dress," I once replied.

I'm extremely allergic to cats. As a little girl, I would pet my cat Baxter and suck my thumb until my eyes swelled shut. As a correspondent I did a segment with a young cancer patient who wanted me to pet her barn cat, so I did. Then we had to do the interview in profile because my eye was so swollen it looked disfigured.

My mom passed her love of books and cats on to Barbara and me, but in many ways we are very different from her, and I think that has a lot to do with opportunity. I wonder sometimes what she might have done with her life if she'd been born a generation later.

One Christmas break early in my marriage, Henry, Barbara, and I went to visit my parents. The whole time we were there, the three of us were fielding work calls and emails. We were staring at our phones most of the day.

At one point, my mother turned to my father and said, "How did we raise such workaholics?" She said it with some measure of pride, fascination, and horror.

When I was growing up, my father was home from work at five or five-thirty every evening. We had dinner as a family every night. We didn't even have a computer until I was in fifth or sixth grade. Even then, we had one only in order to play games like *Where in the World Is Carmen Sandiego?* There were very few distractions during family time. We had uninterrupted conversations, and during meals the phone on the wall went unanswered.

In 1990, my grandmother gave the commencement address at Wellesley College. It later appeared on a list as one of the top fifty speeches of the century. She said: "For several years you've had impressed upon you the importance to your career of dedication and hard work, and, of course, that's true. But as important as your obligations as a doctor, lawyer or business leader will be, you are a human being first, and those human connections with spouses—with children, with friends—are the most important investments you will ever make.

"At the end of your life, you will never regret not having passed one more test, not winning one more verdict or not closing one more deal. You will regret time not spent with a husband, a child, a friend or a parent. . . .

"[I]f you have children—they must come first. You must read to your children, hug your children, and you must love your children. Your success as a family . . . our success as a society depends not on what happens in the White House, but on what happens inside your house."

Because of that speech, many people thought of her as antifeminist. In fact, her entire life she was a strong advocate for women. Her own favorite grandparent, her mother's mother, Lulu Dell Flickinger Robinson, went on a road trip in 1939 through North America with three women friends. Next to a story about J. Edgar Hoover in *The Indianapolis Star* was a headline about the trip: "Mexico Lures Four Widowed Grandmothers."

My great-great-grandmother is quoted as saying, "We believe life begins at sixty."

Looking at my mother, I believe it. She worked for many years as a teacher, a wonderful one. She became a tireless advocate for literacy education and for public libraries. Thanks to her, I've always had my nose in a book. As a girl I adored Betty Smith's *A Tree Grows in Brooklyn,* Louisa May Alcott's *Little Women,* and Toni Morrison's *The Bluest Eye.*

My mother taught E. B. White's *Charlotte's Web* to her third grade class, and she read it to Barbara and me as we snuggled close to her. I still remember some of the lines from that beautiful book: "The early summer days on a farm are the happiest and fairest days of the year. Lilacs bloom and make the air sweet, and then fade. Apple blossoms come with the lilacs, and the bees visit among the apple trees. The days grow warm and soft. School ends, and children have time to play and to fish for trouts in the brook."

I read those same sentences to my girls this year as they leaned against me, taking in every word. As they realized Charlotte was old, they grew worried, but then Poppy said, with certainty, "It's okay. Spiders don't die."

I had to break the news to her that everything dies.

She looked stricken, then asked a question for which I was unprepared: "Even tacos?"

"No, honey!" I said, trying not to laugh. "Tacos have a big place in our home, but they are not alive."

For her family and her generation, my mother's achievements were extraordinary. And yet she once shocked me by saying that she was disappointed her father never pushed her to explore a career. If you were a young woman in 1950s Midland, Texas, you were not expected to work outside the home. The only careers potentially available to you were as a nurse or teacher—both noble professions, of course, but such a small fraction of the roles available to men. My mom told me she did not question those standards until many years later as she watched Barbara and me thrive in our careers. She wondered what she might have been capable of if she'd had more of a push, if more had been expected of her back then.

How strange, I thought. Here I was wishing I felt less pressure from the world while she wished she'd had more.

Her faint regret made me think about what Barbara and I learned from our parents about what path to take. I cast my mind back to the moment when Barbara and I were applying to colleges. As an excellent student, Barbara had her pick. I had far fewer options. One day, though, I believed I had found the answer. In one of the many brochures that my sister had stacked neatly on her desk, full of images of smiling kids in Ivy League T-shirts, I read that Stanford has a special twin policy. If one twin is accepted, the other is automatically accepted as well. Barbara's impressive record would outweigh my mediocre one. She had incredible SAT scores. I had . . . very credible SAT scores, but that no longer mattered! I was going to Stanford!

I snatched up the brochure and ran through the governor's mansion, flapping the glossy pages, saying, "I've got it! I can ride Barbara's coattails to Stanford! They have a twin policy!"

My father caught me mid-flap. "No," he said. "You will absolutely not hurt Barbara's chances at that school or any other school."

Chagrined, I returned to my room. Barbara would go to Yale. I would attend UT Austin. We found our own ways through college and young adulthood.

What did our father want for us? In that moment when he nixed my Stanford scheme, he made it clear. He wanted the same thing his dad had wanted for him: to chart his own course. That had been my grandfather's advice to my darling Mila, too, when she was a newborn, her first summer on earth: "To thine own self be true."

When it comes to my daughters, I would be delighted if they followed in their aunt Barbara's footsteps and became Ivy League graduates. But I would also burst with pride if they turned out like their beautiful, kind Grammee, their houses full of books, cats, and love.

"Every Woman Gets Her Baby in Her Time"

In the wake of my Ganny's and Gampy's deaths, I confided in a friend that sometimes I wished Henry and I were more like my grandparents. I told her how I'd dreamed that our home could be more like theirs in Maine. Their love created a glorious, nurturing base for their children and grandchildren. Entering that house, you just felt joy. *How can I emulate this in my home?* I often thought, watching my girls frolic in Maine during the summer.

"You could do that!" my friend said. "Have a bunch more kids and start hosting holidays."

"Are you kidding?" I said. I explained to her all the ways in which I am not my grandmother. I do not have it in me to have six children. I am unlikely to become the matriarch of a large, close-knit family, one that would want to spend all its holidays together. I can barely keep the stacks of books and projects on my desk from crushing me in a paper avalanche. I don't see myself taping house rules to the back of my guests' doors.

My friend laughed. "You're protesting too much about not having it in you to have more kids," she said. "I bet you're pregnant again within the year."

"Yeah, right!" I said.

Henry and I had no plans to have more children. It wasn't even physically likely. Infertility runs in my family, and it was not easy to conceive Poppy. Now I was three years older, two years into what's termed—rather insultingly, I've always thought—*advanced maternal age.*

What's more, Henry and I, like many parents of young children, struggle to find time to be . . . intimate. One of the many things that can be hard on a marriage with little ones around is that there is always somebody pulling on you, which tends to dampen romantic feelings. It doesn't help that Mila and Poppy are fascinated with my body; nothing caps desire like small children poking at your chest aggressively and screaming, "Boobs!"

No, I told my friend, she was 100 percent wrong in her prediction. If we were to have another baby, it would have to be an immaculate conception.

A FEW WEEKS later, a couple of months after my grandfather's funeral, I was walking down the street and suddenly felt odd. It was an eerie feeling, but one I'd had before . . .

Surely all my symptoms were related to stress. I was busy, and I'd heard I could be in line to replace Kathie Lee Gifford when she announced that she was leaving *Today* after almost eleven years. Just as I was beginning to wonder if that might be an accurate rumor, my boss asked me to lunch. I wondered if he might broach the subject of the promotion, but I decided not to bring it up.

The second we sat down, he offered me the job. Before the waitress even took our orders, he said, "Well, Jenna, I'll cut to the chase. Hoda loves you. We want you to be part of the show."

So many thoughts went through my head in that moment: one was exhilaration. I love the *Today* team. The thought of taking on this new role was thrilling. The next was gratitude. It was a huge vote of confidence. My third emotion, though, was uncertainty.

Throughout our lunch of scallops, my boss talked about the fall TV season, the big changes they had planned. I knew that if my pregnancy suspicion was accurate, sometime in the fall I would be on maternity leave. What if that mattered to my bosses? I didn't *think* it would change things. I couldn't imagine them taking the offer back. But what if they did?

These concerns made me sad, on a personal level and on a political one. It was 2019. I was in a powerful position. I work with terrific people. And still I was worried about my job security because of a baby. Maybe I didn't need to be worried, but I was. I thought about all the women in America who have far more precarious positions than I do who are kept from enjoying something as wonderful as being pregnant.

I put these thoughts out of my head and said yes. He'd asked me if I wanted the job, and I did want the job. This was not the time to try to talk him out of it. We could sort out the details later, baby or no baby.

As soon as I got a chance, I went to the doctor. She told me that I was, indeed, pregnant—about two and a half months along, due in August.

I knew I should have felt joy, but my first feeling was a surge of survivor's guilt. Many of my friends were struggling with infertility. How would they take the news that I was going to have a surprise baby?

When I was visiting my parents in Texas, I told them the news. They were delighted, but the first thing my father said was "Have you told Barbara?" I knew my father worried that Barbara, newly married, would likely be trying soon for a baby if she wasn't already. My parents went through so much in order to conceive us, so they are sensitive to the feelings of anyone who does not yet have the babies they want. They thought that if Barbara was trying, she might understandably envy my pregnancy.

My mother scolded my father for putting that pressure on me. She said what she always says when these questions arise: "Every woman gets her baby in her time."

I reassured my parents that I'd already talked to Barbara and that her reaction had not been to weep for her own childlessness or to begrudge me my happiness. Her official reaction had been to burst out laughing and shout, "Three kids? Holy shit!" (She congratulated me, too.)

I knew that the next person I needed to tell about the pregnancy was Hoda. I fretted over how to do it. She'd worked hard to adopt her baby, Haley Joy, and she desperately wanted Haley to have a baby sister.

As fate would have it, it was International Women's Day when I worked up the courage to ask Hoda if I could speak with her. I closed the door to her dressing room behind me and sat down across from her.

"I have to tell you something," I said. She could see how anxious I was.

She told me to go ahead and say it, whatever it was.

"I'm pregnant," I said. "You're one of the first people I'm telling."

"Oh, thank goodness!" she said. "I thought you were backing out of the show!"

Then she asked me how I felt.

"Scared," I said. "It's a lot all at once. We didn't plan it. And I also feel guilty." I told her what my parents had said about Barbara. And I told her that I'd been praying for Hoda to get her sibling for Haley Joy. "It's hard to get excited for this baby," I said, "when so many of the women in my life don't have the babies they want."

Hoda, tears of unadulterated happiness in her eyes, said, "I'm so happy for you. Truly." She hugged me and asked me more questions.

Her understanding and grace allowed me to begin feeling excited about the pregnancy for the first time.

She also told me not to worry about her. "I haven't told many people," she said, "but I'm in the process of trying to adopt a sister for Haley Joy. I might have news soon."

We held each other and cried, full of relief and full of hope. It was the exact right way to celebrate International Women's Day.

ON THE SUNDAY night before *Hoda and Jenna* was to debut, Henry and I lay in bed watching *60 Minutes*. I had that sleepy Sunday-evening *60 Minutes* feeling. After a weekend with the kids, running around, I was exhausted. Henry left the room for a minute. Before I gave in fully to sleep, I reached over to take a last look at my phone. I peeked at Instagram. The first thing I saw was the new page for our show.

I sat bolt upright. When Henry returned to bed, he said I looked as though I needed a tranquilizer dart. Instead, I FaceTimed my sister and told her about the new logo. It felt real for the first time.

The next morning, having slept for what felt like five minutes, I sat next to Hoda in the makeup chair. She was just as excited as I was.

"Aren't you supposed to be the calm one?" I asked her.

In response, she squealed.

Kathie Lee had left a present in my dressing room. It was a bangle that read "My joy is nonnegotiable." I thought that was the sweetest thing. Then I read the rest of the inscription: "Haley Joy 2017." That is the name and birth year of Hoda's daughter.

I love a regift. I regift often. But that was the first time I've received a gift where I knew who the original gift recipient was! I reregifted the bracelet to Hoda, and the circle was complete. When I told her, Hoda laughed, and we went on to laugh many more times in the course of our first show on what was now our set, hers and mine.

ON A RAINY Sunday evening not long after the show's debut, fate took another turn. I had just returned from Mila's sixth birthday party in Texas, and I was on my way to interview Cher at the Neil Simon Theatre. I had not had anything to eat because the entire flight was spent wrangling the girls. I walked to a Starbucks in Times Square to pick up a snack. In line, I noticed a missed FaceTime call from Hoda. My heart leaped. I wondered if it was the news she had been waiting to hear. I texted her and told her to call me again as soon as she could.

Ever since she told me about her dream of a sister for Haley, I had been praying: *Please let Hoda get her baby. Please let Hoda's baby come to her.* I'd recently begun to go a step further, asking God to *Let Hoda's baby please come before mine.*

Hoda had told me often that when she was with her sister or she saw me with Barbara, she was reminded of how deeply she wanted that same bond for her daughter. I knew it must be hard not to know if or when that new child would arrive. I didn't want her to see any more newborns who were not hers. I did not want her to see me with a baby in my arms if hers were still empty.

I sat down at a back table in Starbucks and saw that Hoda was FaceTiming me again. "Are you alone?" she asked when I picked up the call.

"I'm in Times Square, in a Starbucks," I said, "so sort of the opposite of alone! But I'm in a back corner and I don't think anyone is paying attention to me. What's going on?"

She said, "Do you want to meet baby Hope?"

I burst into tears, and I nodded yes. Looking at Hoda smiling so wide at her perfect little girl, swaddled in her arms, I sat near the restroom in Starbucks and cried. I sobbed until there was not one tear left. If any of the other patrons glanced my way, they must have thought that something was seriously wrong.

I reflected on what my mother had told me: "Every woman gets her baby in her time." It was Hoda's time. Her beautiful baby was here.

In my belly, my baby moved.

How grateful I was that Hoda and I would be doing this all together—creating a new show, she with her baby and me with mine, both our babies right on time. In the depths of sadness and despair around the time of my grandfather's funeral, Henry and I found comfort in each other's arms. Snow had been falling and everyone had been consumed with sadness. Now the sun was shining. For me and for my friend there was new life. Spring had come at last.

"I Learned a Lot from Our Lunch"

I remember so clearly the hours and the months that followed my Ganny's death and how many people's memories of her I heard. The night she died, I lay in bed alone, watching the news. My parents and Henry were in Texas. My girls were sleeping down the hall. Outside, the city was as quiet as it ever gets. From under the covers, I took in one "In Memoriam" segment after another.

Many of the tributes were beautiful. Ganny's voice came through my speakers. "Whether you are talking about education, career or service, you are talking about life . . . ," she said over a montage of images of her as First Lady, "and life really must have joy. It's supposed to be fun!" There she was, glowing on my screen: Ganny as a young woman, as a new mother, and, later, as the matriarch of her large brood, showing the lines of time, a map of life well lived covering her face.

Then came the pundits. Sitting around glass desks in

cold studios, these strangers discussed my grandmother as if they knew her. That first night, the family was too distraught to speak in public. That void was filled by the voices of some people who pretended to have had more access to her than they did. It hurt my heart to hear them.

One talking head said, "We Bush insiders"—I cringed; can you imagine referring to yourself as an insert-family-name-here insider?—"all knew she was going to die first, before her husband."

We knew no such thing! I thought. If anything, we imagined our Gampy would pass first. His health was more fragile, and her dedication to him was strong as steel. *She will die one day after him, of a broken heart,* I always assumed.

Those people on TV, perfectly positioned and clad in camera-friendly shades like cobalt blue, were not filled with malice. Some of them I'd met. But they didn't know her like we did. To see them pontificate in such a blasé way about her death made me feel more alone than I was, and it made me miss her more than I already did. I smiled to imagine what Ganny would say to the woman who uttered so carelessly the line about how we all knew she would die first!

As if to counteract the noise, I scrolled through my phone, looking for her—swiping through pictures and emails we'd exchanged. I made screenshots of countless images of her and reread her emails over and over again, just to hear her voice in my head.

Do you remember when you stuck your tongue out at the press? (In a tribute to my having done that, she once gave me a framed formal portrait of herself, wearing her signature pearls, sticking out her tongue.)

Dear friends for dinner, cocktails first on the deck . . . a glorious night. Thank you so very much. Ganny.

And, so often: *I love you and your precious family.*

The TV screen was full of people speaking of Ganny, the politician's wife. But where was Ganny the grandmother who read to us from our summer reading as the sun set outside our window in Maine? Where was Ganny, the lover of all dogs, even the meanest among them? My girls called Ganny's favorite pets her "bad dogs."

I laughed to remember how one of those bad dogs had bitten a family member in a tender place and held on with all its might. Rather than punish the dog, Ganny scolded the family member for provoking her beloved pet. *Provoking it how?* I wanted to ask her. *With his ass?* But I knew better than to push back on Ganny when it came to her dogs. Politics, yes. Those little hellhounds, no.

I thought back on my grandmother as she really was. I thought of the list of rules Ganny had taped on the doors of every room in their house in Maine. She lived by rules, and yet she was not afraid to break them. I remembered the day at Harry's Bar in Venice, Italy, when she ordered Barbara and me our first martinis. We believed that sipping a martini would bring us our grandmother's elegance and refinement—but we thought it tasted like rubbing alcohol! Straight vodka, we decided, was repulsive! Sorry, Ganny. I know we shouldn't say words like *repulsive*.

I thought about snide, funny comments she had made. I thought of her sitting at our dinner table, opinionated and slightly intimidating, discussing the news of the day. I missed her powerful life force. The world felt less vivid without her in it. With these thoughts swirling in my weary mind, I did what I used to do when I missed Ganny when she was alive: I wrote her a letter, crying as I did so.

Dearest Ganny,

When we lost you, we lost one of the greats. You were our family's rock, the glue that held us together. I hope you know in your final days how many people prayed for you, how many people told me they loved you. It was like that my whole life. People stopped me everywhere—in airports, on the street—and declared their love for you. It always felt good. We didn't mind sharing you with the world.

We called you the "enforcer." It was because, of course, you were a force and you made the rules clear. Your rules: treat everyone equally, don't look down on anyone, use your voices for good, read all the great books. (Oh, how I will miss sharing books with you!) You taught us very early never to say "Yuck," but to politely demur when offered a dish we didn't like and, if pressed, to say, "No, thank you. I don't care for that."

I will never forget when Barbara and I, as seven-year-olds visiting you and Gampy at the White House, snuck to the bowling alley and ordered presidential peanut butter sandwiches. We couldn't wait for someone to deliver what was sure to be the fanciest sandwich of our life. Then you opened the door. You scolded us, telling us that under no circumstances could we order food in the White House like that again. This was not a hotel. You taught us humility and grace.

You and Gampy embodied unconditional love. At our wedding Henry and I asked you to read because we so hoped we could emulate your love story. Your love letters will be passed down to my girls so they know what true devotion looks like.

You always said, "Humor helps." Nights spent sitting around the dinner table in Maine laughing at old family stories were made better because of your laugh. Humor was necessary because of summers surrounded by seventeen raucous grandkids in Kennebunkport. Kids who filled the hot tub with soap, creating a giant bubble bath. Kids who loved doing cannonballs over your head while you peacefully swam laps.

From you, Ganny, I have learned the gift of uniqueness and authenticity: from wearing mismatched Keds to your signature pearls and snow-white hair. You taught us that humor, wit, and grace are the best accessories and that worrying too much about looks is (in your words) boring. Words matter, kindness matters. Looks fade.

In one of your final emails to me you wrote very little. The subject line was simply "YOU." In the body of the email you wrote: "I am watching you. I love you. Ganny."

Well, Ganny, we have spent our lives watching you. We watched as you held babies living with HIV to dispel the stigma, as you championed literacy across our country, as you held Gampy's hand when he got sick.

You always said that you were one of the luckiest women to ever live. But, Gans, I am filled with gratitude because you were ours. We are the lucky ones.

You did things on your own terms up until the very end. . . . And now you are reunited with the little girl I never knew who coined the phrase we still use: Ganny, we love you more than tongue can tell.

Love,

Jenna

I stayed up late, frantically flipping from channel to channel. I was unable to turn away, even when what I saw and heard hurt. All the while, I continued to write to Ganny, using my real memories of her as an antidote to these strangers' theories and opinions. At last I fell asleep, only to dream of her.

GRIEF IS HARD, and I've learned this past year that grieving in public is excruciating. When the person you loved was famous, you must contend, while your pain is at its rawest, with strangers' reactions.

Soon after Ganny's death, a famous political operative wrote on social media that she was "a nasty drunk." It was not just vicious, it was a lie. When she lost her child, in 1953, she went through a bout of depression, but not once in my life had I seen her drunk, nasty or otherwise.

As time passed, I saw a more positive side to grieving for a public figure—people you've never met before coming out of the woodwork to bring you comfort. Walking on the streets of New York City, I was stopped by strangers patting me sympathetically on the arm, grace in their voices as they told me how much my grandmother had meant to them. People I'd never met came up to me and said, "I loved your grandmother." My raw sadness dissipated. Then came healing.

From the eulogies and obituaries, I learned things about her I'd never known, and what I discovered made me proud. She'd showed that she could be supportive of Gampy but also offer her own views without apology. She stood up for what she believed in. I learned that my grandmother was stubborn, but she was also able to change her mind when it mattered.

One article among the many that were published in the wake of my grandmother's death appeared in April 2018 in *The Atlantic,* under the title "Barbara Bush

Changed with Her Country." The writer, Timothy Naftali, described a lunch he had in Maine with her and the
presidential biographer Jon Meacham, during which
the conversation had turned to the issue of transgender
rights.

As First Lady, my grandmother was no stranger to the
gay rights movement. At a time when many politicians
were ignoring the plight of people with AIDS, she hugged
babies and a man with HIV/AIDS in front of cameras.
As a ninety-year-old woman, however, she told Timothy
that she did not understand the big deal being made over
Obama's appointment of a transgender person, nor the
fuss being made about Caitlyn Jenner.

Timothy explained to her how vital it was that transgender people have role models and could witness public
acceptance. He pressed the case with her even though
she seemed resistant. Later he wrote that on the way
home he felt he'd gone too far in his efforts to persuade
her. She was, after all, ninety. Why had he browbeaten
her on this issue?

I understood his passion. I think often of a child from
my first year of teaching. A spunky, funny eight-year-old
whom I'll call Sofia showed up at school in a frilly pink
dress. As soon as her grandmother left after dropping her
off, Sofia quickly ran into the bathroom to change into
board shorts and a big T-shirt.

One day when the children were lining up, girls on
one side, boys on the other, to go to the auditorium for a
spelling competition, Sofia grabbed my hands and tear-

fully said, "Miss Jenna, I don't feel like a girl. I feel like the boys."

"Oh, Sofia!" I said, wiping away her tears. "You go ahead and line up with the boys! From now on, you go in whatever line you want and you wear whatever you want, okay? Now let's go win this spelling bee!" Sofia happily got in the boys' line that day and continued to do so for the rest of the year. If anyone in the class minded, I didn't hear about it.

My colleagues and I met to make sure we were doing everything we could to help Sofia, but we didn't have clear guidelines because it was 2004, long before the current conversation. The National Center for Transgender Equality had been founded only one year earlier. It would be years before transgender people like Chaz Bono, Laverne Cox, and Janet Mock entered the public eye.

I don't know what happened to Sofia. It has been nearly fifteen years since I taught that class. I hope the winds of change brought understanding and acceptance. I pray that Sofia's grandmother packed away the frilly dresses and fiercely loved the grandchild she had rather than the one she'd imagined. I'm glad teachers today know more than I did and have better language for describing the experience of children like Sofia, and that teachers now can point out successful transgender people thriving in the fields of politics, entertainment, sports, and more.

How glad I was to learn that Timothy Naftali made the case about transgender role models to my grandmother. I was sorry to hear that he felt he'd gone too far. But

I was thrilled to read that he later received a message, via a note my grandmother sent to Jon Meacham, saying that she now believed that transgender people were "born that way": "I so enjoyed the lunch and Tim won the argument. . . . Please tell him that at 90 I learned a lot from our lunch. . . ."

In that moment, I saw my grandmother as she really was. I recalled that her seemingly immovable ideas could yield, her unbreakable rules could be bent.

I thought about times I'd argued with her about politics. Why was I so insistent? Why had I challenged the long-held beliefs of a ninety-year-old woman? At that point, who cares who's right? At times my dad had the same experience of arguing a point and then wondering why he hadn't just let the matter drop. We could never resist, though, and that letter she sent to Meacham reminded me of why: because we knew she was listening. We knew she was open to change. Reading that article, I was reminded of the example she set. She taught me that you can always evolve, you can always be better.

I INVITED TIMOTHY Naftali, the author of that article, to my *Today* office at 30 Rock. It was a year after Ganny passed, and I was eager to hear more about their time together. I wanted to tell him what a comfort his article was to me, how it taught me something new about someone I knew so well and missed desperately.

We sat down in my office over cups of coffee and I

asked him how he came to be there that October day in 2015.

Tim said, "Jon Meacham was at the end of the project," meaning Meacham's book, published that year as *Destiny and Power: The American Odyssey of George Herbert Walker Bush.* "Jon said, 'Well, you know, I want to go and say goodbye to the Bushes before they leave Kennebunkport for Houston. Why don't you come with me?'"

Tim found my grandmother in the kitchen, clad in a velour tracksuit. He told me,

> *I kind of sensed that your grandmother wanted to talk. I didn't know her. She wasn't the only First Lady I had met in person. Having worked for the U.S. government, I was well aware of the signals that presidential people send about whether they want to engage or they don't. I walked in and I realized from the beginning that she was open to talking. The first thing she said was about Michael Dukakis and how much she came to appreciate him when she learned about Kitty's depression. I started talking to her about a book I was— and am still—trying to finish on John F. Kennedy. She was very keen about how I was going to deal with the private side of the Kennedy story.*

Then, Tim told me, they moved to the screened-in porch where many vital family conversations had happened over the years. My grandmother's lapdogs, Mini and Bibi, jumped up on the same sofa where I'd sat next to her each summer and discussed what had happened that past year.

Timothy told me he said, "May I pet the dog?"

My grandmother told him, "That dog bites. She's very protective of George and me. If somebody tries to hug us or touch us, the dog will bite them."

Tim said, "Mrs. Bush, there is Secret Service here. I assure you, I'm not going to hug you unless you invite me to!"

She told him, with a mischievous smile, "If I don't like you, I'll ask you to hug me so the dog will bite you."

That's my Ganny, I thought. Conversations with her could feel slightly ribbing, but Tim liked it and played along. He said they had a great dynamic.

My grandparents took Tim and Jon out to eat at a favorite restaurant of the family's. There Tim brought up her work with HIV. He said, "You were really brave to go to that home."

"I wasn't brave," she said. "I had read the research. I knew I couldn't contract it from hugging."

"No, politically you were brave," he said.

She replied, "It isn't courageous to do the right thing."

Those words made me sit up straight. A year after she'd left us, here was a brand-new rule that Ganny lived by and wanted to communicate to others. *You shouldn't get special credit for doing what you should do in the first place.* How typical of her, declining praise and insisting on humility and duty.

Tim became teary-eyed as he sat across from me, recalling their meeting. What struck him most was that she remembered every detail about the man she had met twenty-six years earlier at Grandma's House, a home for people with AIDS. She told Tim about how his Catholic family abandoned him after he came out as gay and HIV positive. Soon Tim and I were both wiping away tears.

Of course, because my grandmother was the topic of conversation, there was laughter, too. Tim told me that at their lunch, when the waiter came by, he had ordered a glass of wine.

"What did you order?" my grandmother asked.

"The house Chardonnay," he said.

She said, "I want to make sure, because recently we came with somebody who ordered a fifty-dollar glass of wine!"

When it came my grandmother's turn to order, she double-checked with the waiter that Tim really did get the house Chardonnay. When the bill came, she checked again!

"That sounds like Ganny," I told Tim, and smiled.

At that lunch, Tim told my grandmother that he had come out as gay later in life. When he told her this, he added that he wished he'd been able to confide in his own grandmother, with whom he'd been close. He told me he felt that in some way, talking about these things with my grandmother gave him a bit of closure. He added that he was happy when a mutual friend of theirs told him that my grandmother had recalled their lunch with great pleasure. "That lunch really changed me," she said.

When Tim got up to leave my office, he said, "Now I'd like to ask you something. Do you feel like you ever changed her mind about anything?"

It was a good question, one I hadn't really pondered.

I reflected for a moment, then replied, "I don't know about that, to be honest. I do know that reading your article changed my mind in an important way. It made me see that my grandmother was able at ninety to change her mind. In this day and age, it seems as though people write one-hundred-and-fifty-word credos and then live by them until they die. No one ever seems to say, 'Maybe I don't know what I'm talking about,' or 'Teach me more.' I love that she was not like that. She wanted to learn. I hope I'm like her."

I saw my Ganny vividly *herself* in Tim's article—doting on her dogs, engaging in debates. To me, there was a lesson in it: if a ninety-year-old woman with strong views on everything could have an open dialogue on a touchy subject, we have no excuse for not keeping our minds open, too.

When my grandmother died and I lay there in bed watching the news, I felt a sense of dread. *How am I going to go through this with all the other people in my family who are public figures?* I wondered. She was the first of those closest to me to receive a period of public mourning, but she will not be the last. When my father dies, will "Bush insiders" weigh in on his character and policy decisions? Yes, they will, probably more divisively than they did when it came to a white-haired First Lady who once gave a speech at Wellesley.

When those terrible days come, I will remind myself of that conversation with Tim and of all those strangers who came up to me to pat my arm. Ganny taught us more than how to die with dignity; she also taught me how to mourn a loved one along with the rest of the world. First, there will be judgment and tears. Then, as time passes, there will be comfort. There will be grace.

Harold

My mother's earliest memory is of peering into the window separating her from the babies in a hospital nursery. There, in a little bassinet, lay her tiny brother, born three months early. My mother was only three years old, but seeing that little boy there so small and weak, she knew he would not live.

Because he was not expected to survive, my uncle was not given the name they had planned for him, Harold Jr., after my Pa. Instead, they named him Edward. When he died just days after his birth, Edward Welch was the name on his gravestone. My Grammee Jenna tried again and again for another baby, but each time she miscarried.

My mother grew up as an only child, but she prayed every single night for a little brother or sister. Sometimes houses feel as full of people who are not there as of those who are. Edward's absence took up space in that house, as did the absence of all the other babies who were never born.

When Barbara and I were young and emboldened by

each other to speak rudely to our mother, she often said by way of scolding that she had never talked to her own parents that way. And it was true. Our mother tried hard throughout her childhood and her adulthood, too, to be the best possible daughter. She wanted to make up for the fact that she was all her parents had. The way she saw it, they had suffered disappointment enough.

THREE YEARS AGO, when I filled in for Kathie Lee on the fourth hour of the *Today* show, one of the guests was Tyler Henry of the TV series *Hollywood Medium,* and I was chosen as the person whose reading he would conduct that day. I was told to bring an object related to a person I loved who had passed. He would give me information about that person on the other side. He was not to be told whose reading he would be doing.

I was skeptical and hoped to fairly test Tyler's abilities. I made sure that the person I had chosen to have contacted—my grandfather Harold Welch—was not all over the internet. There was almost no information available online, as it turned out; he had died before my father was president, before he was even sworn in as governor. In fact, Harold had such a slight presence online that I had to email my mother to request a photo of him.

When Tyler arrived that morning, I was led into a black box and seated in a chair opposite Tyler's chair. The photo from my mother was folded in my pocket.

Right away, Tyler said, "I'm going to go to your mom's side of the family, I think, for some reason. I have an older man that's coming through immediately."

"My grandpa," I said.

"He comes through very strongly," said Tyler. "That's your mom's side, correct? Immediately, as he comes through . . ." Tyler smiled, as if in Pa's presence. "He's so sweet. And he's so connected to you. The first thing he's saying is 'I'm clear mentally.' I don't know why this is coming across."

"He had Alzheimer's," I said. "This is the picture I brought right here." I handed across the photo. "We always thought if we had a boy we would name him after Harold. But we haven't had a boy yet."

"This is a very dignified man, a very proud man," said Tyler. "He's proud of his family. He's a very hardworking man. He's saying, 'To go through this process of losing who I was, that was the hardest part.'"

Tyler saw Harold on a roof. Pa was a home builder. He saw him with babies whom my grandmother had lost. I was impressed that he knew about the miscarriages and stillbirths that had shaped my mom. It seemed to me that either he was a phenomenal researcher or he really did have some kind of sixth sense. I didn't care which it was. I found the conversation incredibly reassuring and cathartic.

"He's referencing Grandma. I don't feel her on the other side. Is she still alive?"

"Yes."

"Nice," said Tyler. "He's making a very special connection to her. He's showing them dancing."

"That's what they did on their first date," I said.

"He's acknowledging that they will be able to dance again someday. When it's her time to go, he will be the first person to welcome her and help her on the other side. There is a reference to two girls. He's talking about two girls since he's passed, so these would have to be your two girls. He does reference to one of them actually seeing him. There was an incident where I feel like I'm seeing little girls babbling and one is looking behind you and that's actually him. He has a connection to your youngest, a very strong one. As far as children, he is referencing that there will be a little boy that will be born."

I had been emotional, but now tears covered my face.

"It's all good," Tyler said to comfort me. "Tears are a release. That's a healing process."

"We loved him so much," I blubbered.

"Of course. And that love continues on. He's still around. And he's at peace."

"So I'm going to have a baby boy? Ahh!"

We had no plans at that time to have a third child. Two were a handful. At the same time, part of me longed for a big family. I loved the idea of a full house. So many couples in my family's past had struggled to have children. This was certainly true of Harold and his wife, Jenna.

Ever since I heard my mother's story about the hospital nursery, I had thought about the name Harold—how neither my mother's parents nor my parents were ever able to use it. It's as though the name Harold had been hovering for decades over our family, waiting for a boy to be born to claim it. I imagined a soul floating out there, waiting for the chance to be named after this giant of a man we all loved.

SOON AFTER I learned I was pregnant with my third child, my doctor told me there were complications. My blood tested positive for what are called Duffy antibodies, which might make my body reject the fetus. Extensive testing would follow, and possibly a blood transfusion. Before we left the doctor's office, she asked if we wanted to know the baby's sex.

I said no without thinking. We didn't find out with Mila; when I was pregnant the first time we did a *Today* show segment in which people guessed. A Chinese healer's pendulum indicated that the baby was a boy, and nearly everyone on set agreed. Al Roker was the only one who got it right. Of course he did. He can predict the weather—he knows these things. But I remembered that when we thought Mila might be a boy, we said we should name him Henry Harold Hager, after Henry and my grandfather, and call him Hal—Hal Hager.

That night after seeing the doctor, Henry and I went out to dinner, our first date night in months. Marriage experts always advise taking weekly date nights. It's very good advice that we routinely ignore. But that night we got a babysitter. We were proud of ourselves, eating together at a restaurant like grown-ups, though in the air were concerns about the baby. To distract ourselves from worrying about whether the baby was healthy, we mused about his or her gender.

Henry's family is filled with girls, just like mine; his brother, Jack, has three daughters and we have two. Our girls have brought us so much happiness. Henry said it still might be nice to bring a boy into the family. He isn't macho in his longing; his girls are his life.

I told him I understood. I love my girls the way they are. And yet when as a child I thought about being a mother, I'd always imagined a houseful of boys. Later, just out of college and working as a teacher, I found myself bonding most with the most precocious, rambunctious boys in my class. Would this new baby be a girl, moving us closer to a full-blown *Little Women* household? Or would this be the first boy for the family in a very long time?

All through dinner, Henry and I kept asking each other, "Should we find out?" We had our doctor's phone number. She'd said we could contact her anytime.

We decided we wanted to know.

As the dessert arrived, I texted our doctor.

Are you sure? she wrote back.

I wrote back, Yes!!

Her reply: one character, a blue heart emoji.

I held my phone up to Henry, then watched as his eyes filled with tears.

Gampy always said tears are healing. He said that we should cry when we're happy and when we're sad and when we're overwhelmed. I thought of him as I, too, felt overcome with emotion. There we were, a married couple dressed up and on a date night, weeping into our cheese-cake. The waitress gave us a wide berth.

If someone had asked in that moment why I was crying, what would I have said?

I don't know that at that moment I could have an-swered, but I see now that I was crying for Henry's par-ents, who would be so happy. I was crying for my girls, who would grow up with a baby brother. I was crying for my parents and my grandparents, who'd never had all the babies they'd hoped for. And I was crying because suddenly there he was, after all these years: a baby named Harold.

April Showers
Bring May Fog

It rained nonstop in April 2019. And it was not lovely warm rain; it was the kind that soaks through your jacket, flies in sideways under your umbrella, and chills your bones. The constant rain and gray skies had convinced me that spring's splendor would never arrive in New York. I was dreaming of hyacinths and praying for sunshine. Instead, I lived in a world of mud and drizzle.

In the first week of May, the rain was still going strong. My mother came to pay a quick visit to Barbara and me and Mila and Poppy. My girls were beside themselves with excitement. I was, too. There is nothing quite like having your mother around when you are pregnant and in need of comfort. So that we would have the most time together possible, I'd talked her into coming on *Today* with me.

The car picked me up at five in the morning. As we drove through the rain-soaked streets of the still-dark city to the studio, I thought, *I hope all this rain is good for the flowers. Where the hell are the flowers, anyway?* I was pregnant, hormonal, and grumpy. The rain matched my dour mood.

Once at work on the set next to my mother, who was beaming and looking graceful in a navy jacket over a white blouse, I shook off the morning's gloom.

We went live and Meredith Vieira asked my mother about the new baby.

"I'm thrilled about the new boy!" she said. "Of course George and I are just thrilled to have another grandchild. As George says, grandchildren are the wonderful part about old age, the *reward* for old age!"

"And you can give them back when you're done," quipped Meredith.

My mom and I joked about how her friends in Texas used to sit around and talk about their medicines. Now they talk about their grandchildren.

Meredith said, "You go from hemorrhoids to grandkids basically!"

My mother, ever the southern lady, said, "Well, we never talked about *those*."

Meredith changed the subject. "What do they call you?"

"Grammee," said my mother. "That's what Barbara and Jenna called my mother and what I called my grandmother." We added that my girls call my father "Jefe," Spanish for "chief."

By the time we walked out of the studio, the weather

had changed. It was now a bright, beautiful day in mid-town Manhattan. At long last, the sun had come out. The sidewalks were packed. I noticed tulips beginning to peek out from the soil on a median and daffodils starting to open in a window box.

"I cannot believe how many people are on the streets," my mother said.

"If you knew how gross the weather has been, you wouldn't be surprised!" I said.

We picked up Mila early from kindergarten. She asked my mom if she could spend the night at her hotel, and my mother said of course. Mila had never been more excited—a sleepover with her grandmother—and on a school night, no less! It was like Christmas in May.

When we got home, Poppy was napping soundly.

My mother kept asking, "When can we wake up Poppy?"

That was just what her father, my Pa, did when we were little girls sleeping in our cribs. He would come to our house in Midland, Texas, fling open our bedroom door, and yell, "Laura, are the girls up yet?"

Our eyes would pop open and we'd yell "Pa!," a word easy for toddlers to learn, then stand up and stretch out our arms, begging him to lift us out of the crib so we could start playing.

I imagine that my mother, a flustered parent of twin girls, wasn't a fan of that method of ending naps, but we loved waking up that way. And now my mother, so much like her own father, doted on her grandchildren. When

I had my back turned for two seconds, I heard Poppy squealing with joy as she woke to find her Grammee and her big sister banging around in her room.

The girls were delighted their grandmother was there to give them undivided attention. They were playing with the vintage Barbie suitcase she'd brought them when my mother's phone rang. It was a family friend in Texas.

"That's funny," my mother said. "I wonder why Elaine is calling."

She took the call into the next room.

"Hello? Elaine?" I heard her say. "Is everything okay?"

Then I heard silence.

"How is she feeling?" my mother said. "Is she eating?" Silence again. Then: "Oh. I see."

She hung up the phone and returned to Mila's room. "I'm sorry, I have to go," she said. "Grammee—my mom—is dying. I need to fetch my bag and get on the next plane to Dallas."

Mila and Poppy both burst into tears. They had met their great-grandmother, but she'd had dementia for a decade, so they never really got to know her as she was.

"Elaine said the end-of-life doctor has come to the retirement community," my mother told me as I tried to console the girls.

What an odd term retirement community *is,* I thought— one often has odd thoughts in moments of crisis. At ninety-nine, Grammee had been retired for forty years. Her mind had been retired for the better part of a decade.

"We were supposed to have a slumber party!" Mila

said, suddenly indignant. "We were going to dinner with Auntie Barbara!"

"Grammee is feeling sad because her mother is sick," I said. "Her mommy needs her. You understand that, don't you?"

Mila did not understand. Like any small child whose promised delights have been withdrawn, she was disappointed. Then she started crying again and said, "Mama, why does everybody we love die?"

Oh, perhaps she did understand. It was a very good question, one for which I did not have an answer. I didn't know what to say.

While my mom rushed to get her things together, Mila called out, "Wait, Grammee! Don't leave! Wait! I need to give you something!"

My mom stood at the elevator door, and Mila ran over, holding out a stick figure drawing of her great-grandma, her name written in lopsided script.

"I want to give you this picture of your mom to make you feel better," Mila said.

My mother hugged her. "Thank you very much, Mila," she said. "I love it, and every time I look at it, I will feel better." Then the elevator doors closed and she was on her way back to Texas.

As soon as she was gone, Poppy broke into hysterical sobs. Lying at the elevator door, she said over and over, "Grammee, Grammee, Grammee."

I carried her to the couch, knowing she had been scared by the urgency she heard in her grandmother's voice. I also knew that she was sad for good reason. Her mom and aunt were about to lose their only living grandparent. Another huge loss—our third in the span of a year.

The next morning on the subway to school, Henry helped Mila send a text to my mom that said:

We love you and your mom. Is she okay? We want to see her in July for her 100th birthday. Love, Mila

The text was decorated with a birthday cake, a cat-face emoji, a little girl, a baby, and a detective.

As I waited to hear from my mother after she landed in Texas, I thought back over Grammee Jenna's life. On her first date with my grandfather, they went dancing at the Tivoli nightclub in Ciudad Juárez, she in a bright red dress. They married at Fort Bliss before he went to war. She never graduated from college, but when she was older she took community college classes until her eyesight failed. When she first developed dementia after Harold died, she cried in the night for her husband, asking where he was. I found some solace in the knowledge that they would soon be reunited.

When Barbara and I were born, our names were assigned alphabetically, perhaps as a nod to my mother's librarian instinct or possibly courtesy of our parents' diplomatic nature. Barbara was named after Ganny because she was the first to emerge. When I appeared only minutes later, I was named Jenna Welch Bush, after my mom's mom.

In those days, we called our grandma Jenna "the nice

one," because in comparison Ganny seemed so strict. There were no rules posted in Grammee Jenna's house. During the day she let us make messes, and at night she taught us all the constellations in the sky. She lay in bed with us, lulling us to sleep with a discussion of our menu for the next morning's breakfast—a meal we always ate outside in sight of the birdfeeders before the day became unbearably hot.

"Let's see," she would say. "We will have apricots and bacon and toast and . . ." We would talk about what the next day would be like as our eyes grew heavy and we drifted off to sleep. At Grammee's house, we always fell asleep excited for the day to come.

In many ways I'm like my Ganny, but I wish I were more like my namesake, Jenna. She was thoughtful and gentle. Watching her brain deteriorate and seeing her lose her radiant curiosity had been painful. But she never lost her kindness. She came to our wedding. Soon after, I went to Midland and sat with her, and she said, "I've got to find you a nice boy!"

"Grammee, you were just at my wedding!" I said.

"There are some nice boys in Midland!" she said, not hearing me. "Who can we introduce you to?"

When she met newborn Mila, she said, "Who is this beautiful baby?" Without ever quite realizing that this was her great-granddaughter, she kept saying, "Pretty baby, pretty baby."

In her later years, she would sometimes look out her window and say, "Do you see those kiddos playing in the yard? Look at those kiddos." Only she saw the playing children.

I wonder now—and maybe it's because I hope it to be true—if those were her babies, the ones she lost, calling her home.

My mom texted me to say the flight had landed and she was heading to the car. She said Grammee was still conscious.

I wonder if Grammee is waiting for you before she lets go, I wrote back.

My mother was her only child. She was her everything. I couldn't help thinking she would want more than anything to say goodbye. While my mother ran to her own mother's side, Mila cuddled up to me and uttered the phrase so often spoken by Robin: "I love you more than tongue can tell."

Saying Goodbye
to Grammee Jenna

It had been a year since we lost our grandmother Barbara. Four seasons had passed without our force, without our matriarch. I still dreamed about her, waking with my eyes filled with tears. And now suddenly it was time to say goodbye to our other grandmother, our sweet, quiet Grammee Jenna.

When our mom called from Texas to tell us that it would only be a matter of hours or days before Grammee died, Barbara and I went for a walk along the cobblestone streets of our New York City neighborhood, leaning into the wind and chill as the sun set over the Hudson.

"Remember when she went down the slide with us?" Barbara asked me.

Our tiny Grammee loved having fun with us, as if she were another kid. She never seemed shocked by the noisy, chaotic ways of young children the way some adults are after too much time apart from them. When we visited her in Midland she never scolded us for being too loud or silly.

"Yes, and remember how she loved baby-food apricots on her toast instead of jam?" I said. "Oh! And that sexy bathtub photo?"

Barbara laughed. The fetching young woman who would become our Grammee Jenna took a seductive picture for Harold, who would become our grandpa. In the photo, which he took with him when he went to fight in World War II, she's in a bath, covered—barely!—by bubbles. This was long before sexting existed. We have always loved this flirtatious image of our beautiful young grandmother, coyly showing off her perfect smile and ivory shoulders.

When we returned to my apartment, Barbara and I did what we had done almost exactly a year before: we picked up the phone to call our dying grandmother. Our grandma Jenna, at ninety-nine years old, was not lucid. By the end of her life she could barely speak.

The landline rang and a voice we recognized as Grammee's devoted nurse, Yolanda Guzman, answered.

"How is she?" I asked.

"She's just so tired," said Yolanda. "She needs to go on and see Harold. Elaine and I keep telling her that it's time. Yesterday she called out for her daddy."

My mom had just been to see her. The only remaining member of Jenna's immediate family, she lay down next to her in bed, just as Grammee had once lain with her daughter and her granddaughters when they were little girls drifting off to sleep. My mom held her mother's once-elegant hand, now paper-thin skin over delicate bones, and soothed her. "Go on, Mom," she told her mother. "Daddy is waiting for you. It's okay to go now."

We knew our grandma couldn't speak. When Barbara and I called her, we did not expect a conversation. We asked Yolanda to hold the phone to her ear.

"We love you, Grammee!" I began. "You were the best grandma in the whole world!"

Were. I meant *are,* but I'd slipped into the past tense, just as I had talking about my other grandmother on TV when she was still alive. Again, the mistake made me wince.

"Go to him," Barbara said after expressing her love and gratitude. "Don't be afraid. Pa is there waiting for you."

I was struck by my sister's astonishing strength. Barbara's beautiful words, her beautiful heart, made me cry. I pictured our grandfather, gone for more than twenty-five years, back in the flush of youth, waiting for our Grammee so they could eat ribs at Johnny's Barbecue, then go out dancing. I imagined him standing on the porch, gray fedora in hand, patiently waiting for her to be done fixing her hair, before he held the door open for her so they could walk together through the warm Texas night.

Barbara and I told her one last time that we loved her, then hung up and hugged each other.

Elaine texted my mother not long after we got off the phone and said, Jenna and Barbara called and she really listened to them. After they hung up, she began letting go.

The next day, our little Grammee died. Barbara and I got on one more plane, to attend the last of our grandparents' funerals.

The service, held on a sunny Texas morning beneath a deep blue tent at the burial site, was quiet and beautiful. A spray of flowers adorned her casket. I leaned over it to say goodbye, wearing a sheer black dress with pink flowers over a black slip, with Barbara by my side in her long-sleeved black dress. Looking at us, tear-stained and placing flowers on the casket, I thought, *Barbara and I have worn black so often in the course of this merciless year.*

There were only a dozen mourners in attendance at Grammee's funeral. When you die at ninety-nine, you've outlived most of the people who love you.

How different this quiet Midland service was from Ganny's in Houston, where more than a thousand people filed in to pay respects. Dignitaries bowed their heads before Ganny's procession. Fans of hers lined the streets, paying homage with signs and candles. A white-robed choir sang. For Grammee, a handful of mourners kept vigil, joined by a chorus of crickets and spring peepers.

I thought back on a photograph of the four of us during my grandmother Barbara's first visit to us in Midland after Barbara and I were born. At the time, Ganny was the wife of the vice president, the Second Lady. Her trip to see her new granddaughters was much publicized. Our grandmothers held their respective namesakes as they stood in the pebbled courtyard of the house we lived in on West Golf Course Road—Ganny in her signature pearls and a purple print dress, holding Barbara; Grammee, wearing a teal sweater and square glasses, proudly holding me.

Now, in the year since both these women have left this earth, I find myself reflecting often on how very different they were from each other. My grandma Barbara went to boarding school and Smith College. My grandma Jenna graduated from El Paso High School and for two years attended the Texas College of Mines and Metallurgy.

Barbara married into an Ivy League family, to a man who would go on to be a congressman, the head of the CIA, vice president, and president. My grandma Jenna married Harold Welch, who after serving in World War II became a home builder. Grammee lived in the modest three-bedroom ranch house he built early in their marriage until she could no longer live safely on her own.

Grammee and Pa were middle-class Democrats. Ganny and Gampy were well-to-do Republicans. By the time we were born, Ganny spoke to crowds beside monuments on the National Mall, while Grammee escaped the heat of Midland by walking for exercise along the slick floors of the Midland Park Mall.

Now they each lay in graves with their husbands. Barbara and George are entombed behind a heavy gate marked with a *B* at his presidential library and museum. Jenna and Harold both rest beneath a plain marble stone, the marker reading, simply, WELCH. He on the left, Harold Bruce; she on the right, Jenna Hawkins, with a small bouquet of bright yellow, pink, and lavender spring flowers between them. My grandpa bought a plot close to the highway, he said, so they could hear the truckers going by.

At Jenna's funeral, I asked my mom, "Do you think Grammee was ever intimidated by Ganny?" (We'd all been daunted by the enforcer at some point. Surely she was not immune to my Ganny's force of will.)

"Not at all," my mother said. Grammee wasn't the type to be intimidated. She had a quiet confidence. She wasn't loud and she didn't boast, but she was proud of her life and her family.

My mother and father chose the readings for Grammee's service. First, my father read Proverbs 31:10–31, the passage about how a good woman is worth more than rubies. Grammee was indeed a good wife, a devoted mother, and an incredible grandmother. My mom said that Barbara and I, her only grandchildren, soothed the place in her heart that had never quite healed after her miscarriages and stillbirths.

My grandmother Barbara gave birth six times and lost one daughter, whose absence defined a huge part of her life. My grandmother Jenna desperately wanted a big, boisterous family. Instead, she had many miscarriages and lost three children in stillbirth. There was a boy when my mom was two, a girl when she was eight, and another girl when my mom was fourteen and my grandma was in her forties. In the end, only my mother survived.

The second reading at the funeral was Psalm 23:1–6. My mother read:

The Lord is my shepherd;
I shall not want.
He makes me lie down in green pastures.
He leads me beside the still waters.
He restores my soul.

As she read, I imagined Grammee reunited in death with her babies. In heaven, she is surely the matriarch she always longed to be.

For the service, I chose a secular text, though to me it is religious in its own way—"In Blackwater Woods," by Mary Oliver, one of my favorite poets. It begins:

Look, the trees
   are turning
   their own bodies
   into pillars

   of light. . . .

To me, this poem is about our Grammee, who paused to appreciate all the little things in nature that others overlooked: a robin's egg cracked open on her back porch, the rocks and wildflowers Barbara and I collected, a particularly exquisite spider's web attached to an old tricycle's handlebars.

When it was Barbara's turn to read, she chose a passage from Ecclesiastes 3:9–11: "What do workers gain from their toil? I have seen the burden God has laid on the human race. He has made everything beautiful in its time. He has also set eternity in the human heart; yet no one can fathom what God has done from beginning to end."

Everything beautiful in its time. I thought back on my grandmother's life, as a young woman taking saucy pictures for her husband in the army, as a mother enchanted with her bookish daughter, as a grandmother so smitten with her granddaughters that she let them stay up past their bedtimes to read them poetry. She was never rushed. You could tell in everything she did that she appreciated the earth beneath her feet and the sky above her head.

At the little lunch after the funeral, I thanked Yolanda and Grammee's other wonderful caregiver, Elaine Magruder, a dear family friend, for all they had done for her in her final years. The contrast between my two grandmothers made me think, too, about women like Yolanda and Elaine, who do so much hard work with so much love and so little fanfare. Yolanda worked with my grandmother for ten years, ever since the dementia hit. Elaine, who looks a bit like my mom, became a surrogate daughter in Grammee's later years. They shared a love of travel and nature. Elaine has said that Grammee helped her notice little treasures in nature the way she did for Barbara and me.

Very few people attended my grandma Jenna's service or saw her obituary in the local paper. That doesn't mean that she wasn't just as important and valuable as my grandmother whom millions mourned. Here is that obituary, so that you may read it and know that when she died a good woman passed from this earth.

Jenna Hawkins Welch, beloved wife, mother, grand-mother, great-grandmother, and friend, passed away on May 10, 2019, in Midland, Texas, at the age of 99. The only child of Jesse and Hal Hawkins, Mrs. Welch was a true daughter of West Texas—a woman who loved its people, its wildlife, and its land. Born on July 24, 1919, in Little Rock, Arkansas, she was raised in Canutillo, outside of El Paso, Texas, one block from the banks of the Rio Grande.

Jenna Hawkins was ten when the Great Depression hit. Almost daily, she watched carloads of Midwesterners and Southerners pass by along Highway 80, fleeing both the Depression and the Dust Bowl for the promise of a better life in California. Her parents ran a "tourist court" of one-room cottages that surrounded a single communal bathroom, where travelers could stop to sleep, shower, and buy a few provisions before moving on.

Jenna Hawkins loved school and reading, a passion she would later nurture in her daughter, Laura. Although she came of age during the Depression, she managed to attend two years of college at the Texas College of Mines and Metallurgy (now the University of Texas at El Paso), before leaving to work full-time.

She was hired by the advertising department of the Popular Dry Goods Company in El Paso. It was there that she met her future husband, Harold Welch. Family lore has it that she looked down from a second-floor office window just as he looked up from the street below.

Harold and Jenna had their first date at Ciudad Juárez's Tivoli nightclub, a few steps from the Mexican-U.S. border. World War II was raging, and there was little time for long romances. Harold and Jenna were married in the chapel on the grounds of the U.S. Army's Fort Bliss in January 1944, just before Master Gunner Harold Welch was shipped out to combat in Europe. He did not return for two years, during which time he was part of the assault on Germany and was among the U.S. forces to liberate the Nazi concentration camp at Nordhausen.

In 1946, not long after Harold's return, the young couple moved from El Paso to Midland, Texas, where on November 4 of that year, their daughter, Laura Lane Welch, the future Mrs. Laura Bush, was born.

Like many women of that era, Jenna Welch stayed home to raise her daughter and make a home for her husband. She devoted considerable time to her main interests: reading and nature.

Her daughter, Laura Bush, recalls coming home from school most afternoons to be "greeted by the soft rustle of pages" and finding her mother immersed in a book. Jenna Welch read aloud to her daughter—

Little Women *was among their favorites—and the two routinely visited the Midland Public Library.*

Mrs. Welch was a knowledgeable, self-taught naturalist. She learned the name of every Midland wildflower and was an accomplished amateur birder. She took extension courses at Midland College and developed a passion for astronomy, which she shared with her daughter and granddaughters. Her daughter remembers how she and her mother would lie on a blanket on the grass and look up at the vast sky. More than two decades later, her twin granddaughters would skywatch with their Grammee.

Jenna Welch engaged in a variety of civic activities, including as a Girl Scout troop leader, a member of the Boone Bible Class and a Sunday school teacher at the First United Methodist Church of Midland, and a member of the Midland Naturalist Society, "the MidNats." In her later years, she lovingly cared for her husband as he battled cancer and later dementia until his death in 1995.

Jenna Hawkins Welch is survived by her daughter, Laura; son-in-law, former President George W. Bush; two granddaughters, Barbara Bush and husband, Craig Coyne, and her namesake, Jenna Hager and husband, Henry Hager; as well as two great-granddaughters. The family would like to thank Elaine Magruder and Yolanda Guzman for their devotion to Mrs. Welch.

A family funeral service was held at Resthaven

Memorial Park in Midland, Texas, on Saturday, May 11. In lieu of flowers, memorial gifts may be made to the Midland County Public Library Foundation, Post Office Box 1634, Midland, Texas, 79702; or to the Jenna Welch Nature Study Center, Post Office Box 2906, Midland, Texas, 79702.

Happy Birthday, Ganny

Dear Ganny,

Today is your ninety-fourth birthday. I woke to a text from Aunt Doro and Dad (like I do every day). Doro wrote:

Today is Mom's birthday. It is happy because Dad is there with her.

I felt a pang of sadness because I had forgotten it was your birthday.

I've begun trying to savor a few minutes of quiet before the rush of each day, time alone to reflect or read. You loved moments like that, too. My favorite part of the day when visiting you in Maine was waking early to come down for coffee—seeing you on the screened-in porch, sipping on your coffee, writing letters and reading. I sat next to you, feeling lucky I had you all to myself.

But I'm sure you of all people can imagine how

time alone—with two little ones—usually turns out. Just a few minutes into my stolen early-morning time, I heard Mila's feet padding down the stairs. (I know I will miss the sound of those small feet rushing toward me one day, though this morning they were an alarm clock ending my reverie!)

As I put my book and coffee cup down and went to give her a hug and to tend to her needs, I remembered how when we were Mila's age all my cousins, Barbara, and I raced to your bedroom first thing in the morning. It was a competition to see who won the most coveted spot on the bed, nestled between you and Gampy. Sometimes I was the victor, and when I snuggled between you, I felt the love you shared. It was tangible, like being in between two lamps giving off heat.

On this perfect blue day in June—you would have loved the weather—as I gave her the first hug of the day, Mila nuzzled close to me, sleep still lingering in her eyes.

"Morning, Mama," her sweet voice said before she gave a huge yawn.

"Morning, Mi," I said. "Guess whose birthday it is today!"

"Whose, Mama?"

"Ganny's!"

"How will we celebrate?" she asked me, suddenly excited. "Do you think she is celebrating in heaven?"

"I think so, Mila," I replied. "I like to think so."

"She's celebrating with Gampy," Mila said with a child's crisp confidence. "And Harold is there, too, at the party with Great-Grammee. Oh, and Robin is there, too, of course, in a pretty dress."

"Yes, Robin is there, too, baby."

"Mama, I'm going to make her a present."

Ganny, you would be ninety-four today. Every other year I can remember, we spent this day in Maine, the oval table surrounded by our throng of aunts, uncles, and raucous cousins. There would be wine and good food and cheers to you, sitting there in your pearls next to Gampy, at the head of the table, smiling ear to ear, holding up your evening Manhattan.

Instead of being with the whole loud bunch in Maine, I'm spending this morning here at home alone with Henry and the girls, everything quiet and still.

So far Mila has not gotten around to making you the present she promised. She became distracted by an unfolding drama involving her Barbies. But she did go outside in her little blue nightgown, to throw a kiss to the perfect morning sky and say, "Happy birthday, Ganny. I love you."

We all love you. Have a wonderful party today. Send our love to Gampy, Pa, Grammee, and Robin. And have a Manhattan for me.

Love,

Jenna

Father's Day
in Maine

Gampy,

It has been four days since Ganny's birthday. And now I have awoken to the first birthday of yours without you here in this world. It is a Wednesday, which means it's a workday and I'm up before dawn, the Manhattan sky still dark, the only time New York feels like a quiet small town. This is my favorite time of the day. It was yours and Ganny's, too.

Late on Ganny's birthday, Henry and I were absent-mindedly talking about the following day and parenting logistics as I scrolled on my phone. I came across a video someone had posted to celebrate her life. It is a video I have watched many times, a tribute to Bob Hope by the two of you. You and Ganny start out reading the script on the teleprompter. Then Ganny slips on a line and you're both soon in hysterics, laughing uncontrollably. You try to redo the speech but end up laughing even harder, your face in your hands.

"Humor helps," I recall Ganny saying.

Henry and I watched that clip and rewatched it. At first we were laughing, and then, overcome with the thought that I will never hear those laughs again, I felt my laughter dissolve into tears. And now again I'm weeping, missing the two of you, your joy, and your uproarious laughter.

Love,

Jenna

We tried to get to Maine as often as possible in that final year of Gampy's life, knowing that any gathering could be our last with him. Losing our grandma had sapped some of his life; she was his enforcer, too.

When we planned his ninety-third birthday dinner, we weren't sure right up until the last minute if my Gampy would be able to attend. After my grandmother passed away, there were times when this once-social man, who commanded every table, would avoid all company, preferring to take his meals on a tray in front of the television in his room, his headphones on, enabling him to hear Mariska Hargitay's voice more clearly as he watched episodes of *Law & Order: SVU.* He was tired. But I also thought it must have been hard for him to sit at the table, my grandmother's empty seat next to him.

As dinner approached and we made preparations, we began to doubt the guest of honor would appear. Then suddenly there he was, dressed sharply in a blue polo shirt, his wheelchair parked at the head of the table, Sully by his side.

The dinner was beautiful. My uncle Marvin and aunt Doro were there, as were my parents and Henry. At the end of the meal, my Gampy blew out the candles on his cake, which read, *Happy 93rd birthday, Dad!* He drank a glass of milk with his slice, just like the children.

AFTER DINNER, AS relatives went off to tuck babies into beds, put dishes in the dishwasher, and walk dogs, my cousin Jebby and I sat at the table with our grandfather. Because of his Parkinson's, sometimes Gampy struggled when speaking. But on this night, he conversed like his old self. With the girls asleep upstairs, I was able to focus on him fully.

"How are you, Gampy?" I asked him once we were sitting quietly. I knew it wasn't a question anyone had asked him lately. I'd seen how difficult it was for my dad and his siblings to see their once-strong father in poor health. They preferred to speak to him about shifts in the tides and the news rather than to dwell on the loss he'd endured or on his fatigue. No one wanted to see our dear Gamps in pain.

"I miss Ganny," he said. He answered the question immediately, and the bluntness of his response shocked me. "I miss her so much. She was a great wife." Then he burst into tears.

The moment he muttered Ganny's name, I, too, began crying. I reached for him and he leaned into my arms. We held each other for a long time, tears soaking our collars.

"Do you think I'll miss her less later?" he asked me, his voice hoarse.

My younger cousin Jebby, always good at leavening the mood, said, "Remember the trips she took us all on when we turned sixteen?" He started telling stories about her, particularly stories about times she'd chewed us out, whether for making a mess, breaking a dish, or borrowing their car without asking.

Soon there was laughter breaking through our tears.

We all thought we were our grandfather's favorite, but Jebby probably really was. He was a great fisherman and spent full summers with them when he was little. Gampy and Jebby had fished all the great rivers together.

We were interrupted by the sound of tiny feet on the stairs. Jebby's daughters, Vivian and Georgia (named after our Gamps), came down to join the party. They kissed Gampy on the cheek, and then Jebby left to put them to bed. My Gampy and I stayed at the table, talking about our Ganny, until all the light had left the sky.

We told story after story—how Ganny had read to us, how she had scolded us, how she had always given us the best advice. How being in Maine without her was hard. How she'd made us better. He asked me about work and about my life, too.

When my grandfather at last went to bed, I found my

dad, telling him, "You're not going to believe it, but I just sat with Gampy for two hours and it was one of the most profound moments of my life. We talked about missing Ganny, how sad it is without her."

"Write it all down," my father said. Of course I didn't. I fell asleep immediately.

Now that I'm back at the house for the very first time without our Gampy, it's all coming back to me. It's Father's Day weekend again—a weekend we have spent for many years in Maine by the sea. I've brought Mila and Poppy. They took their shoes off right by the door, just as Ganny taught them to, and they sprinted into the house, slamming the screen door, calling out, "Grammee! Jefe! We're here!"

As I entered the house, I navigated my way around stacks of boxes. All the belongings from my grandparents' house in Texas had been shipped here. My seventy-two-year-old parents, grandparents themselves, had spent days clad in workout clothes sorting through these boxes and reminiscing. Any box might be filled with precious keepsakes that needed to be extracted from a pile of half-burned candles, torn paperbacks, bent clothes hangers, or dingy baseball caps.

There were piles of things to give to family members and to throw away and to donate. Half the dining room table was covered with dozens of items that didn't quite fit in any pile: a ceramic pig vase, assorted plaques, a Masters golf drink coaster.

"We're here!" Mila called again. The house was

unusually quiet with just my parents and us, instead of the family members who usually came spilling out of every room to greet new arrivals whenever the front door opened.

"Why, hello!" my mother called, emerging from the recesses of the house. As my parents took Mila and Poppy to show them their rooms, I walked around in the strange quiet. The coat closet was still filled with my grandparents' things. A wool coat of Ganny's smelling of mothballs. A pair of fishing waders Gampy hadn't worn in a decade but that still somehow carried the scent of the sea. A goofy red baseball cap with a three-dimensional fish that Gampy wore to make us laugh hung beside one of Ganny's floppy sun hats, worn to keep the sun off her face while she gardened. How odd it felt to see their belongings here without them.

We fell asleep that night in seconds; we were exhausted from the hard work of unpacking and the emotions that being in Maine conjured.

The next morning the girls raced into what was now their grandparents' new room, the one their great-grandparents had lived in for fifty years. Mila and Poppy snuggled in between their Grammee and Jefe, just as Barbara and I once did with Ganny and Gampy as they read the papers. Sitting across from this scene, I was overcome with nostalgia and thoughts about the finite nature of death and the inevitability of change.

My grandparents' La-Z-Boy recliners were gone. Two new chairs—belonging to my parents—sat in their place.

"That's where Great-Gampy used to sit," Mila said. "But it was a different chair, right?

"Yes," she continued, answering her own question as only six-year-olds can. "He sat there next to Great-Ganny, holding her hand."

I had to look away.

Later that morning, as the girls played with their Barbies on the carpet, I read next to my mom in bed as she sifted through the mail, mainly condolence letters from friends and strangers alike, letting her know how deeply sorry they were that she had lost her mother.

"This one is from a friend who was named after Grammee," she said, her eyes misty. "'I was always so proud to be named after her—I carried the name Jenna with such honor,'" my mom read from the letter.

"I feel the same way, Mom," I said. "I love my name now more than ever."

"It has been so hard losing Grammee," my mother said. "Something about the *permanence* of it. I wasn't expecting that to feel so painful. She had been sick for so long. And as Dad says, when your parents die, it reminds you that you're next."

That night I lay in bed in the room I had slept in for a dozen years, with my girls asleep in the room beside mine. The house was silent. Staring at the ceiling, I realized why being in Maine now felt so strange. Not only did I miss Ganny and Gampy, whom I'm reminded of by every piece of furniture and every crash of the waves, but it also reminded me that what my mother said is true—we're next.

The passage of the oldest generation in our family has brought me to a new station in life. I'm no longer the carefree grandchild, running wild with my cousins. No longer are my only obligations hanging up my towels, taking my shoes off by the door, and doing my summer reading. Now I have children, a husband, a career; nieces, nephews, and godchildren. I must wake early to the sounds of my girls, cook pancakes, break up children's arguments, call in to my office. I'm one step closer to being the daughter of ailing parents and then to aging myself.

I'm once more reminded of the passage Barbara read at Grammee's funeral: "What do workers gain from their toil? I have seen the burden God has laid on the human race. He has made everything beautiful in its time. He has also set eternity in the human heart; yet no one can fathom what God has done from beginning to end."

Beginning to end. How recently I was at the beginning. Now I am in the middle. Three of the people I loved most in the world have just reached the end.

Contemplating the beauty and the sorrow, the love and the loss, at last I fell asleep. Outside my window, the sea continued to churn just as it did when I was a little girl scampering over the rocks—and just as it will when, my hair gray, I gaze out the window from my own chair, grandchildren running in and out of the room.

Walking to the Gate

When I was a little girl, on most nights as soon as dinner was over, my Gampy would say, "Who wants to walk to the gate?"

All of us at the children's table would immediately shout, "Me!," tumbling from our seats to find coats and flashlights as the family dogs barked expectantly. Gampy loved this short post-meal stroll, and we loved being with him—a parade of children led by our fearless grandfather, fireflies crisscrossing our path.

LAST AUGUST, AFTER dinner my father was the one to say, "Who wants to walk to the gate?"

From his wheelchair, Gampy surprised us all by saying, "Me!"

We wrapped Gampy in a blanket, and then he, Sully, Barbara, and I joined our father for a walk to the end of the driveway. Mila, who was still awake, threw on my father's vest and joined us, happy to be indoctrinated into the family tradition.

On a perfectly clear August morning, Henry and I drove up the FDR Drive as the sun rose. The time had come to meet our new baby, Henry Harold Hager, whom we planned to call Hal.

When I went into surgery, the doctors were still concerned that the blood type mismatch might cause problems and require a transfusion. But when the baby emerged, he was perfect. As they stitched me back up after the C-section, I cried from relief.

Much was new about this third child. The saddest thing to me was that he was born into a world with no great-grandparents. When Mila and Poppy were born, we FaceTimed Gampy and Ganny from the recovery room. On hearing that Poppy was named after him, my grandfather looked at her with tears rolling down his face.

What remained the same was Barbara and her unstoppable generosity. On hearing the news, she came straight to the hospital, bearing bags of doughnuts and tacos. She was the first relative to hold him. And, once again, she scooted my hospital bed by the window so we could have natural light for our first photos.

The next day, my dad and mom came to meet Hal, bringing the girls with them.

"Daddy would love that there's a little boy named after him," my mother said, gazing at her new grandson.

Mila and Poppy called him a "little munchkin" and sang him songs like "Rock-a-Bye Baby" and "Hush, Little

Walking with Gamps to the gate.

Baby," remembering some of the real lyrics and filling the rest with sung variations of "I do not know the whole song, though . . ."

It had been a few years, but what came back to me right away was that feeling of holding a new life, gazing into the eyes of the family's future. That is the part you never forget—that sense of responsibility, and love, and hope.

And yet, I'd forgotten so much about having a newborn.

Soon I would be reminded of the thumping drone of the breast pump (a noise that sounded to me like the score of the movie *Psycho*), the adult diapers they give you in the hospital, the pain of weaning tempered by cabbage leaves and a too-small sports bra.

After Mila and Poppy were born, we rushed to Maine to show them off to my grandparents. When we took Hal to Maine for the first time, it was a leisurely trip to spend the final weekend of summer with my mom and dad. Walking around the property without my Ganny and Gampy there, I listened to Hal's baby sounds in chorus with the crickets. I thought of how in *Charlotte's Web* "the crickets felt it was their duty to warn everybody that summertime cannot last forever. Even on the most beautiful days in the whole year—the days when summer is changing into fall—the crickets spread the rumor of sadness and change."

Fall—and the next season of sorrow—would surely come. But that weekend it was still summer. Mila and

Poppy were tanned, their feet tough from running around barefoot. Their baby brother was seeing the ocean for the first time. And together we all took the ceremonial post-dinner stroll, walking in silence and pushing Hal in his stroller. The night was warm and quiet as we walked down the driveway. When we reached the end a few minutes later, we paused. It's only about a quarter of a mile, just long enough to see the sun set or to spot the first evening star.

I thought about my grandparents entering heaven's gates and about Marshall Ramsey's image of Ganny's reunion there with Robin. And here were our gates. I touched the cold metal and then turned around.

"Now what?" asked Poppy. It was her first trip to the gate. She didn't quite understand that there was no purpose beyond spending a moment together after a meal and getting a little exercise before bed.

"Now we go back," I said.

She shrugged, turned around, and began trudging back toward the house in the twilight, her ponytail swaying as she went.

This is the life, I thought, echoing the line my mother spoke upon being handed her two babies. This is what life is all about. Until it's your time to enter the gates of heaven and join those in your family who have died, you walk to the gate and then you walk back. You hope that the sky is clear so you can see the moon glowing over the ocean, and you hope always to walk with those you love by your side.

Acknowledgments

This book is about the people I love—who are no longer here. These pages are like love letters to my grandparents, who wrote the profound letters.

It's a book I couldn't have written without guidance from the wonderful people at William Morrow, especially my wonderful editor, Cassie Jones. Thank you everyone who has been so good to this book: Jill Zimmerman, Liate Stehlik, Ben Steinberg, Donna Waitkus, Kelly Rudolph, Kayleigh George, Jeanne Reina, Stephanie Vallejo, Bonni Leon-Berman, and Andrew DiCecco.

I have endless gratitude for my amazing CAA agents: Cait Hoyt and Kate Childs, your creativity and expertise made this project exciting from the start, and having you in my corner made a hard year easier. Thanks also for introducing me to Ada Calhoun, who is a brilliant and compassionate writer and now a dear friend.

To my *Today* team: You made going to work a great joy. Cate Saunders and Gia Maneri: in addition to being full of good ideas, you kept the trains running on time and kept me caffeinated; you are a gift to the world. I wake up (at an ungodly hour!) filled with unmeasurable gratitude that I get to work with some of my best friends. What would I have done this year without Hoda Kotb, and Savannah Guthrie—talk about everything beautiful. I have too many dear friends and family members to mention, but the endless laughter they've given me is the best gift.

Of course, thanks most of all to my precious family: To my parents and grandparents, for teaching me how to live a life of meaning. To my sister, for being my sounding board—and my life partner. And to Henry, Mila, Poppy, and Hal, for filling my days with purpose, love, laughter . . . and endless laundry. I love you more than tongue can tell.